Save the Dudes

Book 1:
The Dudes Adventure Chronicles

By Tyler Reynolds
And Emily Johnson

Epic Spiel Press

This work is a work of fiction. Names, characters, places, and incidents are the product of the author's imagination or are used fictitiously. Any resemblance to actual events, locales, or persons, living or dead, is coincidental.

Text copyright © 2018 Emily Kay Johnson

Cover illustration copyright © 2018 Jacquelyn B. Moore

All Rights Reserved. In accordance with the U.S. Copyright Act of 1976, the scanning, uploading, and electronic sharing of any part of this book without the permission of the publisher is unlawful piracy and theft of the author's intellectual property.

Thank you for your support of the author's rights.

This book is also available as an ebook and audiobook.

Epic Spiel Press

To Owen, Lincoln, and Eric

And to Derek, the original Dude

The Dudes Adventure Chronicles

Save the Dudes

Dudes Take Over

Summer of the Dudes

Dudes in the Middle

Dudes Dog Days

Dudes Hard Target

Check them out at thedudeschronicles.com

Join the Dudes' Readers List at:
https://epicspielpress.emilykayjohnson.com/

Table of Contents

1 Meet the Dudes — *7*
2 Ninja Dudes — *15*
3 Dudes Highway — *22*
4 Dudes Dragnet — *32*
5 Dudes Destiny — *43*
6 Dudes Stealth Mode — *55*
7 Four Dudes and a Girl — *64*
8 Dudes in Trees — *76*
9 Dudes Dojo — *85*
10 Dudes in the Doghouse — *96*
11 Dudes at Work — *102*
12 The Dudes and the Dads — *112*
13 Dudes in the Woods — *124*
14 Dudes Slam Dunk — *133*
15 Dudes at Play — *140*
16 Dudes S-O-S — *150*
17 Dudes Dough Op — *158*
18 Dudes-A-Thon — *169*
19 Dudes Apocalypse — *177*
20 Dudes Deliver — *187*

1 Meet the Dudes

It all started with Operation Wall of Flesh. Ryan got the idea from a video game, and the whole fourth grade agreed because of how the fifth graders were always acting like they ruled the school, or at least the soccer field at recess. And the Dudes are all about doing stuff that's great and memorable (and sticking it to the fifth graders one last time before school was out).

So I was trying to get a selfie with all 82 fourth graders on the swinging bridge of the playground climber--which everyone called the Big Toy. And Ryan was reminding everybody that below us was a river full of hungry crocodiles.

Ryan was even wearing his Indiana Jones hat. Indiana Jones is this guy from a movie his dad showed us one time when the Dudes were hanging around the Maguires's house. That was like a year ago, and you know how it is when you're a little kid and you think everything your parents like is cool. (We're a lot more selective now, of course.) Anyway, the movie is pretty old, but the special effects hold up. After that, Ryan took to wearing a hat.

Anyway, the fifth-graders had stopped their soccer game to come see what was going on. I guess they couldn't get along without any fourth-grade players after all.

Meanwhile, Nate was calculating pressure/density ratios. Deven was making jokes like: "This bridge is so crowded I can't get over it!" And Ryan was yelling at his brother, Connor, not to screw up the plan.

"Connor, get over here!" Ryan demanded.

And Connor obeyed in his usual way by taking a run up the slide like it was a ramp, yelling "Incoming!" and launching himself into our arms like he was a football expecting to be caught.

He was fumbled.

I clicked the camera just as the bridge broke, dumping the whole fourth grade into the "river" of bark chips. Lucky there weren't any real crocodiles. (It was too late to get the picture in the yearbook, but I copied it to the official Dudes Chronicle.)

Ms Nero, the playground monitor ran over, carrying the Disaster Area cones she uses whenever somebody bleeds or throws up. (Which is usually Connor, by the way.)

She shooed the kids away from the Big Toy and declared the whole climber off-limits (even though the bridge was the only thing that was broken). She also put cones around Connor, who was still lying on the ground complaining: "Not cool! Dudes are supposed to stick together."

Lucky it was the last day of school.

Now the summer stretched before us. I was pretty sure Ryan already had some plans for us.

I had a plan too—to keep a record of Dude adventures in the laptop I finally got for my birthday. (It's a hand-me-down from Dad, but I don't mind because I get it all to myself. And, anyway, it still works better than the ones they have at school.)

I wanted to be the one to write the story of the Dudes.

Well, I *wanted* to tell the story to my family, but this is what happened when I tried that night:

"You'll never guess what we did today!" I began. "Ryan had this really cool idea and..."

"Just let me get a burp cloth, honey," my Mom interrupted, edging past me into the living room.

The burp cloth wasn't for me. I have a new baby brother, Leon, who had just finished nursing and was now gnawing on Mom's shoulder.

"Ryan had this great idea to..." I started again, but I was interrupted by a loud hiss as Dad added some liquid to the frying pan. He was cooking dinner.

I waited to start again, but, in the meantime, my middle brother, Jayden, piped up from where he was drawing at the kitchen table.

"Dad! You'll never guess what great idea Jello had today."

"Hmm?" said Dad, frowning at the recipe on his (new) laptop.

"Jello's not even a real name," I complained. "He's making this up to copy me."

1 Meet the Dudes

Jayden had just turned five, so he was now the middle brother. He looked like me, only shorter: blue eyes and brown hair. And he was always copying me.

"I am not!" screamed Jayden. "Dad! Tyler said my story isn't real."

"Tyler, don't say Jayden's story isn't real," said Dad absently. Now he was reading his phone while he stirred.

Mom came back in the room with a cloth over one shoulder and Leon in the crook of her elbow. She frowned at Dad's phone which, of course, Dad didn't notice.

"Hi, Leon!" yelled Jayden at the top of his voice, running over to grab Leon's tiny hand and shake it roughly.

"Careful, honey," said Mom.

Leon was so new he didn't really look like anything yet. He smiled at Jayden and spit up.

I felt the same way.

"Oh!" Mom whipped the cloth off her shoulder and wiped clotted milk off the floor with one hand. Then she flopped down in a kitchen chair and shifted Leon up where he could gnaw on her shoulder again. I could tell it was the same spot because of the milk stains on her shirt.

She looked at me.

"Okay, Jayden, what was it you wanted to say?"

"I'm Tyler!" I said.

Mom sighed wearily. "I'm sorry, honey, that's what I meant."

"Never mind," I told her.

I went to my room and opened my computer. And that's how the Chronicle of the Dudes was born.

Maybe it's for the best. If I could get a word in edgewise at home, I might never have thought of writing about the Dudes and collecting our stories. And you wouldn't be reading this today!

By the way, the Dudes is what we call ourselves when we're together. I'm Tyler Reynolds (the Keeper of the Chronicle). The other guys are: Ryan and Connor Maguire (they're twins, but not the kind that look alike), Nate Howe, and Deven Singh.

We've been together since we were little kids. Ryan and Connor and I were even in preschool together. We

1 Meet the Dudes

met Deven in kindergarten, and Nate's family moved here in first grade.

We see each other at school and scouts, and, if there's a team, we join it together. We five guys live within a couple of blocks of each other too. Dad says that's because they built our neighborhood, Sherwood Heights, behind the school, so people with kids were bound to move in. But I say, being in the same grade and best friends: That's destiny.

I guess you can tell it's been pretty busy at my house since Leon was born. If I didn't have my friends, I'd have no one to talk to. So, as soon as I got to my room that night, I skyped Nate.

"You're lucky," Nate said, rubbing the spot where his glasses always squeezed his nose. "My parents pay *too much* attention. I'm supposed to be practicing my oboe for Junior Symphony right now."

Nate is an only child, which makes him the oldest and the youngest and the middle too. Which, I guess, is why his mom pushes him so hard. She always says, "Whatever you do, do it well." Then she signs him up for everything. She says it's an African American thing because she has to represent her people. But Nate says it's a "Mom" thing because there are lots different "people" at our school, but no other parents represent as hard as she does. Besides, Nate's dad is white, and he's totally on board with the representing plan too, which is what caused our trouble (you'll see what I mean later in the story).

Nate pretty much always does what his parents tell him, which is probably why I could see through the computer's camera that he had his oboe in his hand, a robotics diagram on his music stand, and what looked like a small rocket in his hair. (Nate's hair is super curly, so he tends to stick things in it for safe-keeping. And, being Nate, he also tends to forget about them.)

I said goodbye to Nate and started typing my version of Operation Wall of Flesh while the memories were fresh. I figured the Dudes were destined to be famous. Little did I know that our destiny together was about to be tested that very summer.

2 Ninja Dudes

On the night of the "Welcome Summer" block party, all the Dudes were gathered at my house, which is where the Adventure of the Ninja Dudes begins:

Conner was trying to squeeze into last year's ski pants, and Ryan was pushing his reddish-bald head through a black turtleneck. You'd think it was winter, except for the buzz cuts Mrs. Maguire gave the twins at the beginning of every summer. She said her electric clipper not only saved money but also gave Ryan and Connor less to hold onto during the coming weeks of constant wrestling. Afterward, Ryan, who had reddish-blonde hair always looked kind of bald, whereas Connor's head looked like a cotton swab dipped in orange paint.

"Ninjas did not actually wear black," Nate informed us, watching me wrap mom's winter scarf around my waist.

"They do on *Ninja War*," I said, giving Nate a hard time. It bugs him when we get the details wrong.

Just then, Deven walked in, carrying two grocery bags which he dumped out on the floor with a flourish.

"Whoa! Awesome!" said the guys, pouncing on the mounds of fabric.

"How did you get all these?" I asked.

Deven grinned, a flash of white on his brown face.

"Dude, my mom is Indian and a lawyer," he explained. "She's got loads of scarfs. Anyway, I only brought the black ones."

"These are not all black," said Nate, holding up a long piece of silk with bright pink flowers and black leaves.

"They've got black on them," said Connor, throwing a black and brown striped one over his orange hair.

2 Ninja Dudes

"They'll work," Ryan pronounced, hiding his own hair beneath a knit cap. "Let's hurry up and get ready," he said. "It's almost dark."

It was Ryan's plan, of course. Because of him, the Dudes do stuff other people wouldn't think of doing. (I mean that in a good way.)

We were all into ninjas. (In case you haven't tried them, *Ninja War* videos are awesome.) Ryan and Connor were even going to Ninja Camp at the YMCA this summer. And Nate's mom had him doing an independent research project on ninjas for his advanced reading program.

Yeah, Nate does extra homework. That's how he learned the real scoop on ninjas like how they didn't actually do magic or control the weather like on the show. (Apparently, a lot of the stuff in the show is wrong, although it's still really cool.)

Anyway, everybody agrees that ninjas are sneaky. Tonight, while everyone was at the block party, we were planning to slip out into the dark, where we could practice gliding from shadow to shadow.

So we were covering ourselves from head to toe in black. We were even going to stretch black socks over our sneakers. Our own socks weren't big enough for that, so I went to borrow some out of my Dad's drawer.

That was when Jayden walked in and caught me.

"Hi Jay," I said in a friendly buddy-buddy way. "I'm just helping Mom with the laundry."

Jayden grinned. "I want to help too!" he said.

I should have seen that coming. But I couldn't have him interfering with tonight's mission.

Our neighborhood has this big party every year to kick off summer vacation. Besides the Arts Festival, it's the biggest event of the summer. The grown-ups block off our cul-de-sac, grill burgers and dogs and eat cake decorated to look like the American flag. Ms Kostenko, next door, makes lemonade out of real lemons, and the little kids ride scooters and big wheels.

Every year, the kids play outside until long after dark while the adults chat. Then everyone lies down on blankets and lawn chairs in the road to watch the fireworks, which are set off from the roof of the high school. It was our best chance to sneak around without any of our parents noticing we were gone.

I knew why my little brother wasn't outside with everyone else. (Something about the man-in-the-moon's face freaks him out.) But I needed to get rid of him.

"Jayden, I've got something for you," I told him, heading for the hall closet.

Jay forgot the socks and followed me.

I got out a flashlight and handed it to him.

"This scanner beam will help you patrol the party tonight. Got it?"

"Evil lurks in the dark of night," Jayden said, quoting one of his comic books.

He gave me a thumbs-up, which is kind of hilarious on a preschooler.

"Villains beware!" he shouted. What can I say? The kid has a higher calling.

I listened to the sound of him pounding through the hall and down the stairs. Then the front door slammed and there was silence. Dad was outside at his

SAVE THE DUDES

grill. Mom was probably fussing over Leon. The Dudes had the house to ourselves.

I ducked back into my room and smiled. Four ninjas stared at me out of scarf masks.

"Operation Ninja Prowl is a go, Dudes!" Ryan said, his voice a little muffled.

We were going to climb out my bedroom window, but we didn't know how to remove the screen. So we settled for sneaking ninja-style out the back door and down the deck stairs.

It was not quite dark when we started out. Moving as one, we crossed the back yard and the side-yard and headed for the gap in the hedge between my yard and Ms Kostenko's. She was sure to be at the block party in the cul-de-sac, but we were ninjas, so we wove cautiously from her lilac bush to the rhododendrons that surrounded her gazebo.

Teresa Gutierrez lives right behind Ms Kostenko. She's okay for a girl. By which I mean she has a tree-house and a trampoline, and she always has the latest video games.

When we reached the gazebo, Ryan climbed right up onto the rail and hopped down on the other side of the chain link fence into Teresa's yard. The rest of us followed, but we had no sooner dropped down into the petunia bed than we heard a terrifying noise.

It was a jingling sound, accompanied by high-pitched barking.

For a second, we all froze like the Ninja Warriors do on TV to melt into the background.

Then Nate reminded us, "Dudes! Dogs can *smell* ninjas!"

3 Dude Highway

We all burst out of the flower bed and ran in five directions just as Teacup came scuttling around the side of the house, his license tags swinging.

Teacup was Teresa's Chihuahua. She called him Teacup because he could actually fit into a teacup when he was a puppy. Teresa even had a picture to prove it. But now Teacup was a frightening six inches high and 8 inches long and all yap.

We had to get out of there before the noise got us noticed!

I saw Connor slide across the trampoline, leap the sprinkler, and squeeze through the gate to the front yard like a super ninja.

I ducked under the tree house ladder and followed him—but more like a clumsy panicked ninja.

3 Dude Highway

Deven, Nate and Ryan cut across the patio and ran the other way around the house.

Teacup followed, but Teresa has one of those invisible fence set-ups for the front lawn, so we were safe once we reached the sidewalk.

The Dudes gathered at the end of Teresa's driveway.

Teacup paced the edge of the yard. He was black and tan like a laughably small Doberman. Plus, there was this streak of white down his forehead that gave a perpetually crazed look to his bulging eyes.

Other than Teacup's whining for our blood, Sherwood Drive seemed quiet. If all that barking hadn't brought out the neighbors, they were probably at the block party anyway.

Then Deven broke the silence: "Polka-dot ninja!" he said, pointing at Nate.

Nate had obviously tangled with the snowball bush. There were white petals all over his black clothes. We laughed while Nate removed the clinging petals from his glasses.

Then the light of a car came swinging around the curve, and the five of us tried to scramble behind one tree.

"All right, ninjas, get stealthy," Ryan ordered as he led us into the night.

The real Ninja Warriors have supernatural abilities like being able to turn invisible or summon a storm. But we were almost as good, gliding through the darkness unbeknownst to average citizens.

It was pretty tricky to get around without using the sidewalks though. Sherwood Heights was a maze of cul-de-sacs. It was divided into yards too, and people had fences and hedges. Keeping to the shadows, we cut across the school playground, skirting the broken bridge disaster area. Then we climbed the chain-link fence into Ryan and Connor's yard. From there, we swept down an alley into the next block.

This was another subdivision called Country Club Estates, and it was set apart by a high brick wall that ran around the outside and down between the houses.

Ryan used a handy recycling bin to climb up onto the wall and we all followed: Connor, then me, Nate, and Deven. We could walk along the top, balancing between the backyards like it was our own ninja highway.

About mid-way along we came to a cat who wasn't intimidated by ninjas. It sat like a plump bun on the wall, blinking its green eyes at us. Ryan shoved at it with his foot, but it didn't budge. Finally, he stepped over it.

That was too easy for Connor. Balance is his superpower—that and eating. He laughed and did a cartwheel right over the cat—hand, hand, foot, foot without even touching it. Luckily for the rest of us, Connor's stunt annoyed the cat so much it jumped into the bushes with a flick of its tail and the ninja highway was clear.

I had just passed a backyard with a pool when Deven called, "Hey, guys!" and mimed diving in. Unfortunately, balance is *not* his superpower. Nate had to grab his shirt to keep him from toppling off the wall headfirst.

As we crept along, I could see in the lighted windows of the houses.

Some older ladies were sitting around a fancy living room drinking iced tea.

A man was sacked out in front of a ballgame on tv. (My Grandad sleeps in front of baseball too. I guess that's why they call it "America's Pastime".)

A woman was mopping her kitchen floor, not even guessing we were gliding by in the shadows.

Everything was cool until Ryan got to the end of the wall and found out it was higher than it had been when we got on.

"The neighborhood must be on a slope," said Nate from behind me.

I looked down at the driveway below us—too far below. And there were no helpful recycling bins in sight, just a car parked on the other side of the drive, closer to the next house.

"What do we do?" I whispered.

Ryan leaned around Connor to give us the order. "Go back."

The four of us turned, only to see the whites of Deven's eyes as he careened toward us along the wall.

"I think that lady just saw me!" he said in a frantic whisper.

I looked back over Deven's shoulder to see the porch light come on about three houses back. Two women came out onto the patio. One of them looked our way, and we all froze, hoping we really were invisible in our black clothes.

Her voice carried to us in the stillness. "I'm sure I saw someone, Melba."

"Better safe than sorry," said her companion. "Call the police!"

The Dudes looked at Ryan.

"We've gotta get out of here!" hissed our leader helpfully.

"Well, we can't go *back* now!" said Connor.

Somehow he shrugged past Ryan into the lead position. Then, taking about three running steps, he launched himself off the end of the wall.

It was perfect!

Rather than dropping down onto the cement, he sailed through the air to land running across the hood of the car on the far side of the driveway! We all watched in awe. It was just the kind of thing a Ninja Warrior would have done.

Unfortunately, the first *thump* was followed by enough noise to wake the dead. Connor had triggered the car alarm!

Connor looked up at us, scared, as he slid off the screaming car.

Ryan didn't wait around but took the flying leap himself.

I never would have tried it if the car hadn't been wailing and honking and the lights flashing on and off—it must have been the deluxe model alarm. Anyway, Ryan yelled "Go! Go! Go!"

And I went! Somehow, I made it with only a bruised knee.

Nate had found another way down, lowering himself by his arms until his feet weren't so far from the ground.

I heard a window open overhead and voices which were drowned out by the car alarm as Deven made the final jump and we all hared off out of there. We didn't stop until we had crossed the road and scrambled over the quaint split-rail fence into the Country Club lawn.

Panting, the Dudes hid in a decorative clump of trees. Nearby was a trickling fountain lit with pink lights. A group of bronze deer stood around the fountain sort of looking thirsty. Through the trees I could see cars driving down the Club's driveway, bringing people to some party. I could hear music too, from somewhere nearby.

As soon as he caught his breath, Deven acted out our escape:

"Man, that lady was like: 'By Jove, I think I saw a ninja!'" he said, giving the woman a British accent for some reason. "And Connor was all like: 'Everybody follow me 'cause I can fly!'"

We all laughed. I've noticed before how a terrifying experience helps me appreciate Deven's humor.

"All right, ninjas," Ryan broke in with a serious voice. "We'd better head home before anyone misses us at the block party."

Deven grabbed one of the statues around the neck and said, "What? Leave my *deer* friend?"

SAVE THE DUDES

"Come on, Dev," said Nate, wiping the sweat out of his eyes with the tail end of Deven's mother's scarf. Sweat was rolling down my face too, a combination of the muggy night, the heavy clothes, and all the running.

We plodded back up to Country Club Estates Drive. It was the only road back toward Sherwood Heights, and we couldn't exactly take the ninja highway. We had to walk alongside the driving range where a line of golfers were whacking balls under the floodlights. A tall net protected the road from stray golf balls.

"My dad can do that for hours," said Deven. "It's all about form, son!" he quoted in a decent imitation of his father's stern voice. His arms flailed like a windmill.

Ryan grabbed Deven in a wrestler's hold.

"Don't draw attention," he growled.

"It's unlikely they can see us well," said Nate reassuringly. "The lights are in their eyes, and we're in shadow."

But, just then, a car turned quickly onto Estates Drive, its headlights sweeping toward us. For a moment we were caught in the beams, like squirrels trying to cross a road.

Then I made out the bar of lights on the roof at the same time that Ryan hissed, "It's the cops!" and took off running.

4 Dudes Dragnet

There was only one way to go because of the safety net on one side of the road and the brick wall of Country Club Estates on the other. So we ran forward past the police car and pelted for the corner as fast as we could go.

I knew the cops had seen us because I heard the car stop behind me with a screech and begin to turn around.

The Dudes reached the end of the driving range—that's 500 yards—in about three seconds and flew across the road just as a silver car pulled into the intersection, slammed on its brakes, and laid on the horn.

But they weren't honking at us. The police car, finally having gotten turned around, had tried to follow us and pulled out in front of the silver car. Now the two cars' headlights were pointing at each other, and we Dudes used the distraction to leap into the drainage ditch on the far side of the road.

The ditch water went under Country Club Estates Drive through a big pipe. I knew that, once in the golf course, it became a cute little rocky creek with arched bridges for the golf carts. But right now, it was soaking Dad's socks and leaking into my sneakers.

Ryan, Connor, Nate, Deven, and I all crawled inside the pipe and squatted there under the road, listening to what was happening above:

"Sir, did you see anyone dressed in black come this way?" asked a gruff voice. *(That must be the policeman.)*

"No. I was trying to turn into the country club and found you in my way." *(Annoyed rich guy.)*

"I'm sure I saw them go up Sherwood Road." *(Mistaken younger-sounding cop.)*

"Okay. You can be on your way, sir." *(First cop.)*

"I should think so!" *(Snippy woman passenger. Also rich.)*

The Dudes looked at each other. *(Grinning under our masks.) (Probably.)*

"All right, Racarro," growled the first cop. "Let's do a street-by-street patrol. If they're in Sherwood Heights, we'll find 'em."

Then there were tire sounds as both cars drove away.

"We're the subjects of a manhunt!" said Ryan as we scrambled out of the culvert on the golf course side.

"Cool!" said Connor.

"They're searching our neighborhood," I pointed out. "How are we supposed to get home?"

It was Nate who had the answer. "We cut through the golf course," he said. "The back nine stretches along Sherwood Heights. If we bear Southeast we should find our way *and* avoid the police."

"The fourteenth tee is just a block from my place," Deven put in. "Sometimes my dad sneaks over to play a hole before work." He sniggered. "He's a ninja golfer," he said.

Ryan okayed the plan. "We'll sneak into Deven's house, borrow some clothes, and then saunter over to the Block Party in t-shirts and shorts."

"I'm for that," said Connor as we started out. "I'm melting in these ski pants."

First we had to get past the Clubhouse patio, where people were dancing at a wedding reception or something. It wasn't hard for five ninjas to duck behind the bandstand and some skirted catering tables.

As he crawled by, Deven even reached into a silver bowl and came back with a handful of the club's signature butter mints.

"Don't worry. I'm a member!" he said, passing them out.

The cool mint melted on my tongue as we made our way onto the course and over the rolling hills of short grass. Away from the club's lights we could see stars glimmering in the black sky. Nate was using them to guide our band of adventurers home. What none of us could know then was that getting there would set in motion a course of events that would threaten the very existence of the Dudes and cause us to question the fate that brought us together.

In a few minutes, we could see the screen of trees meant to prevent golf balls from breaking people's windows in Sherwood Heights. But, when we reached the fourteenth tee, we saw something else: the police car! It was blocking the end of Sherwood Court. And it looked like all our friends and neighbors had left the block party to crowd around.

The older cop seemed to be addressing the crowd.

"Probably telling them to be on the lookout for five short robbers wearing black," said Connor.

"Now what?" I asked. "We'll never sneak into Deven's without being seen."

"We wait," said Ryan calmly.

He led us back over to the tee where we wouldn't be seen from the road. "The police won't hang around forever," he assured us. "And the fireworks will start soon. All we have to do is wait until everyone is looking up, and..."

His next words were drowned, literally, by a heavy spray of water!

You know how you're walking along the sidewalk and you come to a yard with the sprinkler on and you jump to the side to escape? Well, each of the Dudes jumped, all right, but there was no escape! There were high-powered sprinklers all over the golf course, apparently set to come on at ten. It was like being in a car wash.

I grinned at Nate through the scarf over my face.

"I thought you said ninjas can't really summon storms," I teased.

Water was streaming down his glasses, so he took them off and squinted at me.

"I seem to have been mistaken," he said.

Then there was a *pop*, and we looked up, and the fireworks had started. They were being set off from the roof of the high school, which isn't too far, so there were bursts of light right over our heads.

Deven was the first to peel off his wet shirt with a *whoop*. Then the rest of us followed.

When Connor got rid of his soggy ski pants, we just laughed and stripped down to our underwear too. It felt great to be free of the hot, sweaty clothes at last.

The water was cool, and the fireworks were amazing...

Until I noticed other lights—flashlights—approaching up the hill from the Clubhouse.

"Uh, guys..." I said.

I saw two figures stop for a minute at what must have been a control valve. Then the sprinklers died. But the flashlight beams kept playing up the hill. We knew they'd seen us.

Connor grabbed at the nearest pile of clothing, but there was no way we could get those soggy rags back on.

Then Nate, thinking fast (which is really the only speed he has), took all the black clothes and tossed them in the bushes.

A minute later, we were in the company of two Country Club security guards.

I glanced down as they moved the beams of their flashlights from one to the other of us. At least we all had colored underwear—the long kind that sort of looks like shorts or could maybe pass for a swimsuit if it's pretty dark out and nobody looks too close.

Which the security guards weren't doing. They seemed a little embarrassed to have caught a bunch of half-dressed boys on the fourteenth tee. They were even more embarrassed to walk us home—or rather to the cul-de-sac, where the block party was breaking up.

The fireworks had ended by now, so there was nothing to distract people from getting a load of us in our wet underwear—which we kept insisting were swimsuits.

(Of course, our parents didn't jump in to contradict us. Deven's mom even went out the next day and bought him a pair of swim trunks the same turquoise as his underwear to reinforce the lie whenever he swam in the Country Club pool.)

Speaking of pools, Nate's dad went off the deep end. Apparently, getting arrested for indecent exposure was the kind of thing that could tank your college applications—not that we were actually arrested—or indecent.

Nate kept his mouth shut as his parents shared a look over his head.

"This is just the kind of thing I've been afraid of," said Nate's mom (like she could have guessed this would happen!).

The movement of her perfect red lipstick drew the eye like a poisonous snake fascinating its prey as Mrs. Howe said to her husband, "Maybe now you'll listen to me about sending Nate to private school."

"This is not the future we want for our son," agreed Mr. Howe. "I'll call Einstein Academy tomorrow for an appointment."

After that, our parents led us away to our separate homes to change our underwear.

It was all over the <u>Sherwood News</u> online the next morning—not our underwear, the ninjas.

MYSTERIOUS BLACK-CLAD PROWLERS

GANG OF THIEVES THWARTED BY SHERWOOD POLICE.

(Which just goes to show that you can't believe everything you read online.)

"You know, I think Jayden spotted one of them last night," Mom told me at breakfast. "When the police came over, he told them all about it, didn't you, honey?"

"Yeah," said Jayden. "There was a bad guy in Mrs. Stinko's yard."

"Kostenko, dear," Mom corrected. She pulled Jayden into her lap.

"My flashlight saw him but he ran!" said Jayden, wiggling out of Mom's arms.

Mom said, "They were probably looking to rob houses while everyone was out at the block party."

"Sounds like an inside job," Dad said, jiggling Leon. (He didn't know how right he was.)

"It's a good thing our police were on the ball," Mom added.

Dad grinned at Leon before passing him to Mom. Then he pinned me with his serious look—which was sort of undercut by the blob of spit-up now soaking into his work shirt.

"You missed the police visit, Tyler," Dad said. "We need to have a talk about you boys going off on your own like that." He covered the spit-up with his jacket.

I started to explain, "See, Ryan had this great idea..."

"Right now I've got to get to the airport," Dad interrupted, glancing at his watch. "We'll have to talk when I get back."

"Sure, Dad," I said with a sigh. Luckily, Dad's attention span isn't that long. But I still wished he wasn't going on another work trip. It seemed like Dad was never around when I had something cool to tell him.

I went to my room to write my own version of last night in the Chronicles. Somebody would probably want to know the real story someday.

5 Dudes Destiny

Nate's mom didn't want him getting involved with the police. "She says they might make a dangerous mistake," he told me.

"That's funny," I said. "My parents think the police are great, except when Dad gets a ticket rushing to the airport."

"That's because you're white," Nate explained.

"I guess," I agreed. "But it's not fair that black kids can't do just as much stupid stuff as anybody else. Plus, you didn't look any blacker than the rest of us last night. Which reminds me, we have to go get the wet clothes."

"I can't come with you," Nate said mournfully. "I have to go with my parents to check out Einstein Academy."

My dad said Mr. Howe had talked about that school before. Dad and Mr. Howe were friends in college. Now they live in the same neighborhood and work at the same company, and their sons are best friends. I would call that destiny, but Dad says that's him telling his friend about a job opening.

"Make your own destiny, son," he always says. "That's what you have to do in this world."

Only now Mr. and Mrs. Howe were trying to change Nate's destiny—and break up the Dudes too.

The rest of the Dudes and I went over to the 14th tee after breakfast.

"Dude, my dad teed off right here this morning," said Deven.

"Good thing he didn't look in the bushes and see this stuff," said Connor, lifting a damp wad of cloth.

"You've got to concentrate," mimicked Deven, waving a branch like a crooked golf club. "Pay no attention to the rubbish in the shrubbery!"

"Mr. Howe was pretty ticked last night," Connor remembered.

"Did you see how his glasses fogged up?" Deven put in. "Those security guards were like: 'Please don't kill us for arresting your soggy son. We were only taking him to golf jail!'"

"Nate's been at Sherwood School since first grade," I said, over the laughter. "And Mrs. Howe is the president of the PTA."

"Right," Connor agreed. "Einstein Academy is all the way across town. They probably won't even like it."

"Don't worry, guys," said Ryan confidently. "Nate's parents will cool down and change their minds. Now, pick up those wet clothes," he ordered his brother.

Connor picked them up all right, and socked Ryan in the face with a wet scarf, beginning another Maguire wrestling match.

"Bam! Right in the kisser," began Deven's play-by-play:

"Now they're down. Now they're up. Now Ryan's got Connor in a head-lock. It doesn't look good—

seriously, folks. It doesn't look good," Deven snapped. "I've never seen Connor's face that color!"

I tried to laugh, but I couldn't help worrying (about Nate, not Connor). Parents make a lot of dumb decisions that their kids have to live with. Obviously, Ryan and Connor weren't happy when their dad moved out last year. And I wasn't thrilled that my parents decided to have another baby. Now Nate's parents were talking about breaking up the Dudes!

Anyway, just about the time Connor had gotten a foot in Ryan's stomach we heard the bell from their place. Their mom has this big dinner bell she uses to summon them from all over the neighborhood so she doesn't have to call all the dudes' parents and ask where her kids are.

Ryan and Connor headed home.

I helped Deven carry the wet clothes to his house. His grandmother lived with him, and he assured me she would take care of the laundry.

"The greatest thing about Nani is, she doesn't ask questions," Deven said, kissing her cheek and taking the lunch sack she handed him.

"Come over as soon as you can after camp!" I told him as I left.

Ryan and Connor and Deven were in YMCA Ninja Camp together. I had to miss out just because Mom was home for the summer taking care of Leon.

"You used to complain about going to YMCA," said Mom.

"All my friends are there," I told her. (Well, all except Nate.) "There's nothing to do at home."

Mom sighed, "I wish I had your problem," she said, settling Leon down on his belly in the middle of a baby blanket on the floor. She called it "tummy time" and treated it like serious exercise, even though he mostly just lay there.

"Why don't you and Jayden keep Leon entertained until I'm done with the dishes," she suggested, "and then maybe we can do something together."

I shrugged and sat down next to the baby blanket.

Leon didn't really do much at this age. He wasn't even interested in toys. He could barely raise his head to give you a goofy look.

Jayden got down on the floor too and laid his head about an inch from Leon's face.

"You're gonna warp his mind," I warned.

But Jayden started in on this freaky baby language he'd invented.

"El-lah, ittle-lah bab-wah!" said Jayden.

I had to look away. There was the TV, hanging dark and lonely on the wall.

"Mom!" I called. "Can we watch the Ninja War marathon?"

I heard the water stop in the kitchen. "Didn't you already see all the episodes?" she called back.

"Yeah, but…"

"How long is it?" she asked, coming to the doorway wiping her hands on a towel.

"I don't know," I said, not liking the third degree. "It's a marathon, so…"

"Record it and watch one a day," she said, smiling like she'd invented burritos or something.

"One a day!" I protested.

"You and Jayden don't need that much screen time," she said. "And Leon doesn't need *any*."

She glanced fondly toward where Jayden and Leon were giving each other the fish-eye.

Screen time was a thing with Mom. She actually thought everything with a screen—TV, cellphone, computer, whatever—was bad for young minds. It was oppressive.

I had to be careful to save enough screen time to type in the Chronicles—priorities, you know? Which wasn't really fair because Dad uses a computer all day long, and so did Mom when she was working.

Mom came over and put a hand on my head, smoothing the hair out of my eyes the way she always did.

"You've got a whole summer with no school," she said. "You want to spend it *doing*, not just watching."

Maybe she had a point. I didn't want to use up all the episodes the first day. So I turned it around on her.

"You've got the whole summer off work," I pointed out. "What are *you* going to do?"

She laughed. "Oh, I think my plans are laid out for me," she said, gesturing at the pile of laundry on the couch—which just goes to show it was *her* mind that was damaged.

I remembered the last time Mom took off from work—five years ago now. It was right after she had Jayden. We had spent his naptimes reading together—Harry Potter and <u>The Hobbit,</u> <u>The Chronicles of Narnia,</u> <u>The Chronicles of Prydain</u>...Come to think of it, maybe that was where I got the idea to write a chronicle for the Dudes.

Mom picked up a shirt so tiny it didn't seem worth folding.

"Why don't you tell me about Ninja Wars," she said. "What's so great about this show?"

I grinned. "Okay," I said. "So it starts like this: Hiro's uncle dies, and he inherits the old man's house which is way up a mountainside. Only, when he gets there..."

Just about that time, Leon started to fuss in his whiny, screechy way.

Mom dropped the laundry and my story.

"I told him he shouldn't eat that," said Jayden.

"Eat what?!" Mom gasped, scooping Leon off the floor. "What did he eat, Jayden?" she demanded.

"His booger," Jayden explained. "You're not supposed to eat boogers," he said virtuously, "so I was trying to scrape it off his face."

While Mom dabbed Leon's face with a wipe, Jayden turned to me. "I think he really wanted that booger," he said.

I rolled my eyes. Come to think of it, Jayden had interrupted me a lot when *he* was the baby. Now they were both doing it. It really didn't pay to be the oldest.

"Leon's just fussy because he needs his nap," said Mom. "I'd better go put him down."

Of course, I had learned that when Mom said "put him down," she meant "hold him until he falls asleep—or until your father comes home, whichever comes first."

Dad was on a plane to Cleveland, so this could take a while.

"Come on, Jayden. "Let's go outside," I said, pausing first to set the DVR.

SAVE THE DUDES

We got out the dart guns, assembled all their special attachments and loaded them all. Then we argued over who would get to use the Raider 8 with the night scope, which is the best gun even though the Stealth Attack can hold more ammo if you have all the clips, which I don't yet.

Anyway, Jayden only likes the Raider 8 because 8 is his favorite number. (Go figure five-year-olds.)

So I pretended to want the Infinity Blast Revolver, which, incidentally, I *don't* favor because it shoots two darts at a time so you're always out of ammo and you never hit anything anyway. But the infinity symbol on its stock looks like a sideways 8, so Jayden loves it. And he got jealous the minute I wanted it, just like I knew he would.

So, after all that, Jayden took the Infinity Blast with the Sniper as back-up and I took the Raider 8 with the Destroyer as back-up, and we had a battle for about thirty seconds until all the darts were lost in the bushes.

Then I tried to get Jayden to collect them for me. But he wouldn't because he actually likes using *pretend* ammo better than darts. So, for the rest of the morning he followed me around, pointing his finger and making noises that caused spit to fly out of his mouth.

We watched Ninja Wars, ep 1 at lunch. Mom even made mac-n-cheese from a box, which is our favorite delicacy.

I thought she might get to like the show, but about half-way through, she heard Leon screeching through the baby monitor. She had to go change his diaper and missed the whole "summoning the storm" scene.

I chuckled, remembering the sprinklers last night.

"What's so funny, Tyler?" Jayden asked.

"Nothing," I replied, turning off the tv. "Let's do Legos."

We keep the Legos in the basement so Leon doesn't eat any—not that he could swallow anything irreplaceable, but better safe than sorry.

In the basement, I was reminded of my sleepover last year. (Some of the stains were still visible in the carpet.)

That night, Nate had been obsessed with building something mysterious and intricate out of Legos. He missed the burp opera and the donut eating contest

(Connor won). Not even Deven's impression of a chicken doing the hula could disturb him (and it disturbed me plenty). I woke once in the wee hours to see Nate sitting on his sleeping bag, putting bricks together with his eyes closed.

In the morning, his creation had still looked pretty random.

Then Nate told us it was a replica of the battle of Stalingrad. And, all of a sudden, I could look past the primary colors to see little overturned tanks and gun emplacements and trenches and burned out buildings, exactly to scale. It was cool in a Nate kind of way, even if he did take apart my Y-wing fighter to do it. Nate even videoed it in black and white so it would look like vintage film on his youtube channel.

I hoped Nate was going to hate his tour of Einstein Academy.

6 Dudes Stealth Mode

The other Dudes, except Nate, came over right after camp.

Mom had put tape over our doorbell to keep delivery men from waking the baby, so Ryan, Connor, and Deven walked through the flower bed to the living room window and cupped their hands around their faces to peer in.

Mom jumped when she saw them.

"You'll have to play quietly," she told us skeptically as she let them in.

"Don't worry, Mrs. Reynolds," Ryan assured her. "Ninjas are all about stealth."

Unfortunately, Connor chose that moment to loudly crunch an apple, and Deven balled up a rattle-y fruit snacks wrapper and made a jump-shot for the trash basket.

Before mom could say anything her phone rang, and she scrambled to answer it before the chirping could wake Leon.

"Your mom would be The Dragon," said Ryan as Mom walked out of the room.

"Definitely," Connor agreed, flopping down on the couch.

"What do you mean?" I asked.

"We got codenames at camp," Ryan explained.

"You use a codename that reminds you of the person so you can remember easier," Connor interrupted him. Having finished his apple, he set the core on the couch and picked up the baby monitor.

"It's animals and plants, mostly," said Ryan.

"I'm Monkey because I climb a lot," Connor put in, tossing the baby monitor from hand to hand.

"Yeah, and I'm Tiger," Ryan said. "And I don't know why Deven is Chicken."

"Because I was dancing like this when they were giving out codenames," Deven explained, giving a demonstration.

We all nodded.

Mom interrupted us by wandering back into the room.

"Who told you to call me?" she said into the phone. With the phone wedged against her shoulder, she folded three dishtowels from the laundry basket while she listened to the answer.

"Well, I don't...Oh," she said, dropping a towel. "Yes, I *am* at home this summer. I suppose I could... Okay, Trudy. If you really think so. I'll see you then."

I perked up my ears as Mom hung up.

"That was Nate's mother," she said, confirming my guess.

Mom frowned around the room as if she expected Nate to be here spying on her. "Someone told her I'm home for the summer," she said. "And now she wants me on some committee to fix the school playground. Trudy even says she's grooming me to *take over* for her as president of the PTA!" Mom looked as shell-shocked as I felt.

Nate's mom volunteered at the school *a lot*. In fact she was there more than some of the teachers. She'd been president of the PTA for the last three years running. If she was giving it up...

"Gosh, Mrs. Reynolds," said Ryan. "You'd think Mrs. Howe wouldn't want Nate to leave Sherwood School after all her hard work making it decent."

Mom sighed. "Forget Nate," she said. "I don't want *Trudy* to leave me with all that work!"

At least Mom was on our side.

Or maybe not:

"I'd like to get my hands on whoever broke that bridge on the playground...," she muttered, stalking back to the kitchen.

When she was gone, I said, "I guess the Howes must have *liked* Einstein Academy."

"Nate's doomed!" wailed Deven.

"Not yet," Ryan assured us. "We'll come up with a plan to change Nate's fate. But we'll have to keep it top secret," he said.

We all fell silent as Mom walked through. Absently, she took the baby monitor from Connor's hands, sponged it off with a baby wipe and set it back on the coffee table. Then she grabbed the apple core off the couch cushion, wrapped it in the wipe, and tossed it in the trash on her way out of the room.

When she was gone, Ryan said, "The first thing we'd better do is put the whole operation in code."

I could see his point. The Dudes didn't have a clubhouse or anything. We tended to hang out at whoever's house had the least nagging and the most snacks. That would naturally be Ryan and Connor's house except that we weren't allowed to play there when Mrs. Maguire was at work. And there was nowhere else that didn't have adult supervision, which is the grown up word for eavesdropping.

"We'll call it Operation Destiny," Ryan decided as we gathered around.

It had a poetic ring, I thought.

"Ninja code sounds like poetry," Connor confirmed. "Like 'a cloud strays across the moon' means your target is hidden. Or..."

"Nate's really smart," Ryan cut in, "so he's gotta be some really smart animal, like..."

"Like an owl!" Connor finished.

"Of course," said Ryan, giving his twin the evil eye. "That's what *I* was gonna say. And Mrs. Howe could be..."

"A bee, right?" said Connor, cutting him off. "Because of how she's so busy and buzzing around Nate all the time and kinda scary..."

"Fine, a bee!" Ryan snapped. Then he said, "Connor, why don't you *demonstrate* how the codes work?"

Connor jumped up but halted mid-leap. "Huh?" he said.

"Go away," Ryan suggested with a smile. "I mean, go do some spying and report back in code. Later."

Connor's eyes gleamed as he went into stealth mode and slunk out of the room.

When Connor was gone, Ryan was free to tell us more stuff he learned at ninja camp like how to silently subdue a foe.

"With karate chops?" said Jayden. He chopped a bin of baby toys which bounced and rattled.

Like a shot, Mom rushed in, grabbed the bin, and whisked it out of striking range.

"Nah," said Ryan when she was gone. "For some reason, they don't let us hit each other at camp. But they taught us how to make a blow-gun."

Deven tore off pieces of Jayden's coloring book and demonstrated how to roll the tube and how to make a spit-ball to put in it.

While he did this, Ryan explained, "Of course, a real ninja would use a dart with Sleeping Lotus Potion. A blow-gun is the perfect spy weapon. If anybody catches you, you just unroll the piece of paper and there's no weapon to find."

There was a flaw in that scenario, and Mom found it when she came back and caught Deven in mid blow.

Her eyes widened.

"Did you just blow a spitball at my wall?" she asked, like Deven had just smacked her baby or something.

We all looked at the ninja "dart" where it had splatted by the fireplace. "Sleeping Lotus Potion" had spattered out from its sides on impact.

Mom's face turned red. "*Why* did you do that?" she demanded. Then she looked again. "And why is it *purple*?!"

"The fruit snacks were grape," Deven answered sheepishly.

Mom's codename was a good one because I'm pretty sure she was about to start breathing fire. But, suddenly, she stopped and turned her head to listen. Mom was super-sensitive to noise these days, and, sure enough, there was a faint sound coming from the baby monitor. But it wasn't Leon's screechy whine.

"What *is* that?" asked Mom, picking up the monitor from the coffee table.

That's when we heard the whisper of Connor's voice saying: *"The melon is in the basket. Repeat. The melon is in the basket."*

"Is someone up in the baby's room?" asked Mom, doing a quick head count.

"It's a code, Mom," crowed Jayden happily. "You're the dragon!"

Mom didn't respond, just set the monitor down firmly on the table and marched up the stairs.

6 Dudes Stealth Mode

As soon as she was out of sight, Deven lunged for the monitor. "The dragon is smoking!" he hissed uselessly into the speaker. "The dragon is smoking!"

"Dude, that's not a walkie-talkie," I told him.

To tell the truth, Connor had learned his stealth lessons well. Leon would never have woken up and screamed if Mom hadn't charged into the nursery like some medieval beast.

But it didn't matter. After that, the Dudes weren't allowed inside the house during Leon's nap. If we wanted to make a plan to save Nate, we'd have to find somewhere else to do it.

7 Four Dudes and A Girl

"I know," said Ryan the next afternoon. "Let's go over to Teresa's."

That wasn't as surprising as you might think. Teresa is the kind of girl who has Ninja War II on the Game System. Besides that, Jayden wasn't allowed to leave the yard, so it saved us from the finger gun too.

Teresa's mom invited us in. She's a principal over at the middle school so she was home for the summer. Teresa even shut Teacup in her room so we could hang out in the den.

Ryan and Deven called "first challenge!" the minute we walked in, and Connor and I called "second".

"Go ahead," said Teresa graciously. "Since you're guests, I'll wait and defeat whoever survives."

7 Four Dudes and a Girl

While Connor and I awaited our turn to fight to the death, we let Teresa show us her less-yappy pets. She had fish in light-up tanks around the room. Some of the fish were light-up too, I think. Also, she had a guinea pig and a frog and something called "Sweetie" that stayed under his rock the whole time we were there.

Mrs. Gutierrez served us lemonade and cheese curls, which was nice. But we couldn't say a word about Operation Destiny because she kept hanging around like she had nothing better to do than remind us to keep our feet off the furniture.

Nate missed the whole thing, of course. He had an oboe lesson.

"Nate has a different camp or lesson every day," I complained that night over dinner. "We hardly get to see him as it is. And now his parents are talking about sending him to private school."

SAVE THE DUDES

I'd had an email from him that afternoon. It had said Einstein Academy was "okay." Whatever that means.

I also got one from my dad. Apparently Cleveland is "okay" too.

Mom finished chewing her crockpot lasagna before she spoke.

"Honey, Einstein Academy might be good for Nate," she said. "Maybe you should try to be happy for him."

But I wasn't happy about it. And I didn't think Nate was either. If only the Dudes could get Nate's parents to see that they were making a mistake.

"Eat your lasagna, Jayden," said Mom.

Jayden made a face.

"You like noodles," she reminded him.

"They've got sauce," Jayden reminded her.

The kid had a point. I was old enough to trust Mom's lasagna, but unfamiliar sauce *could* cloak vegetables or other nasty surprises.

Mom stood and picked up Jayden's plate.

7 Four Dudes and a Girl

"Einstein Academy has a good reputation," she said over her shoulder to me while she washed Jayden's noodles at the sink. "If Nate gets in, his parents won't turn down the opportunity."

Mom handed the plate back to Jayden as she said, "I just wish Trudy hadn't picked on me for the playground committee. Now I have to spend Leon's naptimes making phone calls."

"Look mom!" called Jayden. He was slurping wet noodles into his mouth like floppy tongues.

Mom sighed. "Every mother wants her children to make the most of their abilities," she said, adding, "Nate's mom just wants the best for Nate."

The *Dudes* knew what was best for Nate, I thought. We just had to prove it.

The next afternoon, Nate had a rocket workshop—whatever that is. But, the rest of us went back to Teresa's.

This time, Mrs. Gutierrez served lemonade on the patio outside and said there would be no video games today. I guess she heard somewhere about the "dangers" of screen time.

Maybe it was just as well. We hadn't gotten much done yesterday—aside from getting pwned by Teresa in the Shadowblade Tournament. We needed somewhere without parents or distractions to discuss Nate's situation.

Right then Teresa said, "Wanna go in my tree house?"

Teresa's tree house is like a real house in a tree, but it's kinda girly. It has pink walls and hinged shutters and a slanting green roof. The balcony railing is a white picket fence.

Inside there are things painted on the walls, so it looks like you're in a house with furniture, only everything is flat. It was a pretty good trick, because Deven kept trying to sit on the sofa and sliding down the wall.

"My uncle painted all this," Teresa informed us. "He went to art school and he's even named after a famous artist: Miguelangel—like Michelangelo!"

7 Four Dudes and a Girl

We stayed anyway. At least Teacup was too small to climb the ladder, so he couldn't chew Ryan's leg.

We tried to pretend Teresa wasn't there, but it wasn't easy. Her bubblegum lip-gloss was smelling up the place. And the one room was kinda crowded with her *and* all the Dudes—well, all but Nate.

"Hey guys," I said, "we've got to talk about Operation Destiny."

"Huh?" said Deven.

"What's Operation Destiny?" asked Teresa all bright and nosy.

Ryan puffed out his chest.

"It's a secret plan, Teresa," he said importantly. "Ninja stuff. I'm sorry, but, if you insist on staying, we're going to have to talk in code."

Teresa narrowed her eyes. "It's *my* treehouse," she said.

Ryan looked at me, and I shrugged.

"Okay," Ryan ordered the Dudes, "this mission is classified, so everybody talk in code around Teresa."

"Right," I said. Deven and Connor nodded.

While Teresa turned her back and pretended to do her hair in front of the painted mirror on the wall, Ryan got right to the point: "You guys know that, uh, *something bad* is going to happen to uh, *somebody*."

"Who?" asked Deven.

"*You* know," said Ryan meaningfully.

"Who! Who!" hooted Deven, and Ryan relaxed.

"Right. The Owl," he said.

"What?" asked Connor, causing Ryan to thump him on the head.

Teresa was now bending to smell the painted flowers on the painted end table, but I could tell it was just an act. She was listening all right.

"The Owl may have to go to a private...nest," said Ryan. "It's across town—I mean, the *forest*. We have to stop it. We have to keep him in Sherwood!"

"We could shake the tree," said Connor. "Or knock the nest down with a rock."

"Yeah!" said Deven. "Let's burn the nest. Or tear it up and stomp on it!"

I sensed we were having code problems.

7 Four Dudes and a Girl

Ryan sighed. "You want to get us arrested? The nest is..." He stopped himself as Teresa crossed to the window and leaned out looking down.

I could hear faint whining that must be coming from Teacup in the yard below.

"We can't do anything to the nest, okay?" Ryan told the guys. "Forget the nest."

"The nest doesn't matter anyway," I put in. "What matters is...Seal Harbor."

I had chosen this code name because Sherwood School's mascot was a seal named Sammy. But would the other Dudes understand? At this point, Teresa looked the least confused of any of us, and she was blowing kisses to a dog.

"We've got to make *Seal Harbor* look like a wonderful opportunity for the *Owl*," I tried to explain, "better than any *private nest*."

"We could say it's got more fish!" suggested Connor.

I hesitated, unsure whether "fish" was code or just a reference to the cafeteria's fish sticks, which Connor had been known to eat in record numbers.

But Teresa seemed convinced. "More fish!" she gasped suddenly. "I'd better call Uncle Miguelangel right away," she said, scrambling out the door and down the ladder.

"That was weird," said Connor when she was gone.

Ryan dismissed it with a shrug. "Girls," he said.

"Never mind Teresa," I said. "We've got to convince the Bee that Seal Harbor is a great place to raise an Owl!" (There's something I never thought I'd hear myself say.)

Then Deven asked, "What about the Red-necked Gecko?"

"Aggh!" roared Connor, pulling his hair. "Can we talk English for a while?" he begged.

"*I* don't even know who the gecko is," said Ryan.

Deven grinned. "Remember when Nate's dad was talking to the golf cops and his neck got so red?"

We all cracked up. Mr. Howe would totally look like a gecko if you took away his nerdy glasses.

"We'll have to work on Mr. Howe too," said Ryan. "We'll show him the Owl needs to stay right here."

Right about then Teresa returned.

7 Four Dudes and a Girl

"Sorry we have to keep you in the dark on this, Teresa," Ryan told her. "It's top secret."

"Oh I know exactly what you've been talking about, Ryan Maguire," she said. "And you don't have to worry about the Owl. He'll be there with his costume."

"What costume?" I said.

"Be where?" Ryan asked.

"The Arts Festival of course," Teresa answered, "just like he always is. I told my uncle to offer Art more money so he won't book that private event."

Oh yeah, right. Art the Owl was the mascot of the annual Arts Festival in town. He wears a costume and peers at the art with his enormous eyes. (Corny, I know.)

But now Ryan and I grinned at each other because Teresa was obviously way off track.

Teresa folded her arms. "You see? I know all about it, so you can cut out the code talk now."

"Yeah, you got us, Teresa," said Ryan with a wink. "We've got a secret about the Arts Festival, and you figured it out." (I guess Art the Owl owed us one for getting him a raise.)

"We'd better stop talking in code around you," I added. And I wasn't kidding. I mean, this whole discussion would have been a lot easier without Teresa listening in.

"You should have come to me in the first place," she said. "Uncle Miguelangel will do anything for his favorite niece, and he's pretty much in charge of the whole Sherwood Arts Committee."

"Is that the same guy who painted all this junk on the walls?" Ryan asked.

Right away, Teresa swelled up like he'd paid her a real compliment. (I've noticed it's pretty much impossible to insult her.)

"Uncle Miguelangel *built* this tree house too," she said proudly. "He's a contractor, and he knows what he's doing."

"I thought you said he was an artist," I said.

"How do you think he paid for art school?" said Teresa. "He built this treehouse in one day."

Then Ryan said, "He didn't have time to build furniture, I guess, so he had to paint it on. Lucky your dad's got a paint store."

7 Four Dudes and a Girl

Teresa just smiled primly. She was proud of her dad's paint store too, I guess.

I could see Teresa's happiness was rubbing Ryan the wrong way. We really couldn't get anything done with her around. I was wishing, again, that the Dudes had a place of our own when destiny came flying out of Teresa's mouth.

"It's too bad you boys don't have a tree house of your own," she said.

"We could build one as well as your uncle—better even," Ryan said.

"You could not," said Teresa. Then she licked at her lip gloss and added, "Not in one day, like Uncle Miguelangel, anyway."

Well, we all knew what that meant.

"Come on, guys," said Ryan. "We'll build ourselves a tree house, and it's not gonna be pink either!"

"What's wrong with pink?" asked Connor, but Ryan was already dragging him toward the ladder.

8 Dudes In Trees

As we left Teresa's house, Connor asked, "How are we gonna build a tree house? We don't even have any big trees in our yard."

"We don't want to build it there anyway, dufus," said Ryan. "Mom would just worry that you'd fall and break your neck—'Connor baby'."

Of course, this started another fight.

Luckily, I didn't have to guess which way to turn when we got to the sidewalk. I was pretty sure we would build the Dudes' tree house in *my* back yard—so Teresa could see it.

We had the trees for it. Along my back fence there was a row of old crabapple trees, with big branching arms close enough to the ground to reach but high enough so we'd still need a ladder—which is kinda the point.

We knew they were sturdy enough. Connor had climbed them several times over the years and never fallen out...at least not because of a broken branch.

There's an old shed in the back yard too. It came with the house. The way my mom tells it, she and Dad didn't ask old Mr. Dorminter what was in the shed when they bought the place. They were just so anxious to get a house in this neighborhood. Mom was already pregnant with me, and Dad had a new job. So, after they moved in, they never had time to really check it out.

I had been in there a few times looking for a mouse to keep as a pet. From what I had seen, it looked like Mr. Dorminter must have been into woodworking—sort of.

My grandpa has a wood-shop in his garage. Granddad keeps wood of different kinds stacked on racks so it doesn't warp. He has a vacuum to pick up sawdust and all the tools hang on little hooks.

Mr. Dorminter's shed wasn't like that. It was just full of wood. Most of it was two-by-fours cut to odd lengths and leaning against the walls. But there were wider pieces and short chunks. All of it looked like it had been used a few times with old nail holes and hammer dents and splashes of paint in different colors.

In a bucket on the floor we found a couple hammers and a rusty saw and some screwdrivers. In a jar on the windowsill were what looked like all the bent nails that had been pulled out and half-way straightened.

"What's with the bouncy floor?" said Deven.

Sure enough, the floor was three layers thick with big pieces of plywood that must have been used—and warped—before. We tried walking around to flatten them a little, which didn't work. Then Ryan declared it good enough.

"Let's start building!"

The four of us got to work pulling boards out of the shed one by one and nailing them to the trees. We didn't have blueprints or anything. Each dude just put boards where he thought it looked like they needed to go.

We'd barely gotten started when Mom came out with the baby on her hip to see what we were up to. Jayden trotted across the grass after her.

"Where did you get all these...things?" she asked.

"A lot of it was in the shed," I told her.

"Yeah, Mrs. Reynolds," said Ryan, "we cleaned out your shed for you!"

Mom's forehead furrowed like she was trying to think of something wrong with us using a bunch of rusty tools to hang rotten wood in the trees.

"Don't leave any nails in the yard for when your father mows the grass," Mom warned.

She held Leon up to see his big brother hammering. He smiled his toothless grin and didn't mind the banging at all. Sometimes I thought he was going to grow up to be an all right brother.

"I wanna see!" said Jayden, begging to be picked up.

"You can see from there, Jay," said Mom, her arms already full.

"No I can't," insisted Jayden, reaching toward her.

"I'll lift you up, little dude!" said Ryan.

He dropped his hammer and grabbed Jayden around the middle, swinging him around.

Jayden squealed with laughter.

It didn't bother me to see Ryan getting along with my little brother. I just happened to say, "Come on, guys. Let's get back to work."

Connor took a different approach to get his brother's attention.

"Got your hammer!" he called, snatching the tool from the ground.

"Hey! I was using that," yelled Ryan, dropping Jay.

"Come inside, Jayden," said Mom nervously, averting her eyes from where Connor was now climbing to the highest part of the tree with a hammer in his teeth and Ryan was standing right under him, shaking his fist.

"Try to keep it down, boys," Mom called from the deck. "I have to call some playground companies. They never have prices on their websites," she complained as she shut the sliding door.

8 Dudes in Trees

Deven has a phone so his grandmother can call him home in the afternoon when her "programs" are over. (Screen time! I'm just saying.) I guess it's a high-tech version of the Maguires's dinner bell.

By the time Nani called for Deven to come home and get cleaned up for supper, we had a pretty decent floor—actually three separate plywood floors braced between the branches of the three crabapple trees. Not quite sure how that happened.

They were a little tilt-y because Mr. Dorminter didn't have a level. And they were still a little bouncy because of the warping.

"That will work itself out," said Ryan knowledgably.

He nailed three chunks of wood to the trunk of the first tree to make a ladder. Then we spent time scrambling from tree to tree. From the first platform, we discovered you could balance along a branch to the next. To get to the third platform, it looked like you had to leap a "chasm", but, if you were in the know, you could grab the branch above and swing across, which was pretty cool.

We couldn't wait to show Nate.

When Nate finally came over after Chess Club on Thursday, he was pleased.

"This is better than the outdoor classroom at Einstein Academy," he said.

"What's that?" I asked.

"It's some benches in a circle in the woods outside their science lab," he explained.

"Sounds dumb," said Ryan fiercely.

Nate shrugged. "Their science lab is cool, but not as cool as this."

He pulled a pencil out of his hair and a chess tournament flier out of his pocket and started sketching something.

Teresa wasn't nearly as impressed when she saw our treehouse from her trampoline. "This is all you got done yesterday?" she called across the fence from the peak of a bounce.

From somewhere in the petunias, Teacup growled at Ryan.

"Better hold onto that mutt of yours," Ryan growled back. "I wouldn't want anything *violent* to happen to him."

Teacup stuck his nose in the corner of the fence like he wanted to get a piece of Ryan—a small piece, of course.

On her next bounce, Teresa looked critically at the tree house platforms. "Where are the walls?" she asked, doing a somersault.

It was just like Teresa to point out the wall situation. And it was unfair too. After all, we had really made *three* tree houses in one day—if you only counted floors. And now we were out of wood. Plus, and most importantly, we'd been down a man. Nate probably would have had some great ideas for walls if he'd been around when we were building.

Ryan knew just what to say, of course.

"We don't *want* walls!" he declared.

Teresa's dog-ears flew up in the air like she was surprised. On her next bounce, she asked the worst possible question: "Why?"

Our side of the fence was silent.

I wracked my brain, trying to think of *any* reason for building a tree house without walls.

That's when good old Nate spoke up.

"Ryan is right," he said. "These platforms are part of a training system we are designing to hone our balance, strength and skill."

"Huh?" said Deven, looking at Nate.

"What does that mean?" asked Teresa, crossing her arms in the air.

But I was beginning to get the picture. Balance, Strength, and Skill were the elements always being perfected by the Battle Ninjas on Ninja Wars. Their sensei insisted on it.

"It means," said Nate, holding up his sketch, which was really a set of plans, "we are building a dojo."

Now you know why he's the Owl.

9 Dudes Dojo

On Friday morning, the PTA's Playground Committee met in our living room.

At the same time, the Dudes' Committee to Save the Owl met in the back yard. We were preparing a surprise for Nate's mother.

Ryan figured that making ourselves an awesome dojo just happened to be a great way to show Mrs. Howe that Nate didn't need private school.

"Mom says I need projects and people who engage and enrich my creativity," said Nate.

Ryan nodded. "That's why I'm putting you in charge of the whole thing!"

Nate had already designed tests of strength, skill, and balance to turn our ordinary treehouse into a tri-level dojo. All we had to do was build them. The lack of walls would give us plenty of elbow-room for martial arts. (So there, Teresa!)

While the playground committee drank coffee and crunched numbers, the Dudes spent the morning on dojo construction.

My job was to fill an old burlap sack we found in the shed. Nate wanted it layered with balled up plastic grocery sacks and nearly a whole ten-pound bag of flour. When I asked what that was for, he did his best impression of an evil genius laugh.

(Sometimes I wonder about Nate.)

Then he said, "I'm going to need something from home."

He put on his helmet with the rearview mirrors and his day-glow vest with the reflective stripes (yeah, his mom's a little overprotective) and rode off on his bike.

While he was gone, I thought about what Mom had said about Nate making the most of his abilities. I'm the first to admit Nate has a great mind. And it was always working too. Just like his mom, Nate always had a project.

For instance, right now, I knew, in between music lessons and science camps, he was working on a way to power an automatic dart gun with your shoes instead of batteries.

I was pretty sure Nate would figure it out eventually.

Then Ryan would come up with an awesome battle plan.

Connor's jumps and stunts would provide us a source of unlimited power.

Deven would make us all die laughing while the darts were flying.

And I—well, I would write about it so future generations would remember that it all started with the Dudes.

It seemed to me Nate couldn't make the most of his abilities anywhere else. But it was his parents we needed to convince. I hoped building a dojo would look a lot more "engaging and enriching" than sitting on benches in the woods at Einstein Academy.

When Nate came back from his house, he had a new set of pulleys still in the box.

"We need rope," he said.

So Ryan walked Connor over wrapped in coils of heavy rope from their garage.

"These are Dad's," Ryan explained, unwinding his brother, "from when he used to take us camping."

Deven ran home too and brought an old badminton set, some flower pots, and a plaster garden gnome which he wheeled over in his dad's yard cart.

"Look! It's our sensei!" he joked, bowing to the gnome.

Nate picked up a badminton racket.

"I can use these," he said, "the cart too."

"Go ahead," said Deven. "Dad gave up gardening. He's got a new hobby now: yelling at the high school kid he hired to take care of the grass."

Everything else we needed we could scrounge from Mr. Dorminter's shed.

When we were finished, we had kind of an obstacle course where five ninja could hone their balance, strength and skill on three different levels of the tree house. Nate explained the challenges and Ryan came up with a cool ninja name for each one:

Move the Mountain was a test of strength. You had to use a rope and pulleys to hoist a board piled with stuff to the second platform.

"The pulleys trade force for distance," Nate explained.

But we changed the name to **Drunken Deadweight** after the board tilted and a flower pot fell off. It would have broken if it hadn't landed on Connor's shoe.

"It'd be better with a weight that can hold on," said Connor, hopping around the yard on one foot.

"Yeah," said Ryan. "Tyler, where's your brother?"

The Rain of Blows tested balance and agility. Nate had duct-taped the badminton rackets to the net poles and then attached them to one wheel of the yard cart, which he skewered on an old mop handle stuck in the ground. When the wheel turned, the ninja on the first platform had to jump the spinning rackets to avoid getting whacked.

We also tied a rope between the highest tree and the shed. Nate had rigged a handle onto one of the pulleys so you could start on the third platform, lift your legs, and use it as a zip line. You just had to be sure to catch yourself with your feet to prevent splatting your face on the shed wall. Ryan called that **The Flying Kick**.

The Blades of Death were a pair of Mr. Dorminter's rusty grass clippers. If you flung them just right toward the flower bed, they would spin end over end and stick straight down into the soft, weedy ground like a throwing star.

But my favorite was the **Accursed Enemy**. This was my burlap sack, swinging and bobbing as someone raised and lowered it on another pulley. The ninja's task was to use his best moves to whale on it (and keep from being "sacked" himself). You could even try it blindfolded to build your night-fighting skills.

If you landed a punch or kick, a bunch of flour would oof out of the sides of the bag. That was just for effect, but it looked awesome.

When we had tried out all the challenges, Ryan whacked an old pot lid we were using as a gong.

"I now pronounce this Ninja Dojo open!" he said. "Let the training begin!"

9 Dudes Dojo

We were all bowing to the garden gnome when Mom and Mrs. Howe came out on the deck. Their meeting must be over. Mom held Leon, who fussed a little, squinting as they stepped into the sunshine.

"What's all this?" Mom asked. "I thought you were finished building your tree house."

"It's a dojo now, Mrs. Reynolds," supplied Ryan, helpfully.

"What's a dojo?" Mom asked.

"It's a place for training ninja," Nate explained.

"Nate did an independent research project on ninjas this year," said Mrs. Howe proudly.

Mom shaded her eyes and peered into the shadows under the trees.

"Is this about that tv show?" she asked suspiciously.

"We've been playing *outside* all day, Mom," I said, adding for Mrs. Howe's benefit, "because it's healthy!"

"And we've been learning about how pulleys work," put in Ryan.

"Yeah. They trade forks for difference," said Deven.

"Force for distance," I corrected quickly.

"Very good," said Mrs. Howe. She looked impressed. "And I like that you're getting your vitamin D from the sun," she added.

Mom smiled as Jayden rushed down the deck steps and across the yard. She turned to Mrs. Howe and said, "I wish Jayden would spend a little more time outside."

"Yeah," said Deven, eyeing my brother. "The little guy's getting spots!"

It was true. There were streaks and splashes of blue and red on Jayden's face, and green and yellow on his shirt and hands.

Mom chuckled. "That's just paint," she said. "Jayden was bored, so I got him a paint set to keep him occupied during the meeting."

That was typical. When I'm bored I'm supposed to "make my own fun." Jayden gets a present. (I think I've said this before, but it doesn't pay to be the oldest.)

"It's important to encourage the arts," said Mrs. Howe approvingly.

I saw Mrs. Howe looking at her watch and realized we needed to draw her attention back to Nate and the dojo.

"Nate designed a whole training regimen for us," I explained, "to improve our balance strength and skill." I gave the badminton rackets a spin.

Nate got whacked on the shins once or twice, but then he got the rhythm.

"The Rain of Blows!" I announced with a flourish.

Leon was hypnotized by the spinning rackets—an unexpected benefit.

"That looks like good exercise," said Mrs. Howe.

Then Connor yelled, "The Flying Kick!"

Both moms gasped as Connor flew down the zip line into the shed wall with a resounding *boom*.

Mrs. Howe averted her eyes from Connor in time to shriek as Deven threw the Blades of Death with amazing accuracy, managing to whack a big branch off Mom's hosta plant.

"Boys, don't..." Mom started, but ended with a cry when she saw Jayden rising from the ground as the

Drunken Deadweight. (It *did* work better with a weight that could hold on!)

Both mothers watched, spellbound, as Ryan raised my brother fifteen feet in the air, took one hand off the rope to wave, then lowered him safely to the ground.

"Whee! Now its Leon's turn," offered Jayden generously.

I saw Mom flinch, but Ryan said, "Nah. He's too light."

"The Accursed Enemy!" I announced, whirling to give the burlap bag an especially powerful chop that sent flour puffing into the air.

Unfortunately, Nate was standing a little too close and caught a face full of flour.

"What do you think, Mom?" he said, coughing and peering through the white haze.

"I think we need to leave," said Mrs. Howe. "Quickly," she added.

Then she turned to my mom and tapped her watch. "I've got to go, Meg. Nate has his admissions test today, and we want to be on time. I'll call you later about the playground bridge."

The admissions test! I grabbed Nate's arm while he was wiping the flour off his glasses.

"Remember," I whispered. "They can't make you go to private school if you don't get in."

Nate nodded before putting his glasses on over his pasty face and following his mom out of the yard.

10 Dudes In the Doghouse

Mom used her sweetest voice to ask, "Honey, can you watch your little brothers this morning while I make a few phone calls?"

Usually it takes more than her "sweet" voice to make me responsible for Jayden. But, this time, I knew the phone calls were for the PTA playground committee, so I was cool about it. I was thinking that, if the swinging bridge got replaced, Nate's mom would be pleased and maybe forget about Einstein Academy.

Anyway, Jayden wasn't so much trouble today. He was sitting at the kitchen table doing paintings for the Arts Festival—one after the other. From what I could tell, Jayden had done seventeen paintings in the last five minutes alone. If he was any good as an artist, the kid was going to make a fortune someday.

Of course, they all looked the same to me—every color in the paint tray swirled together with the same brush until there was a brownish blob and sometimes a hole in the center of the paper. At least it was keeping him occupied. That way Leon could get some uninterrupted time with his biggest—and best—brother.

"Now, Leon," I said, opening the Foam Dart Company website on my laptop. "I'm gonna show you why the Boomzooka is better in a fire-fight than the Mega Mortar."

I never talked down to Leon the way the rest of the family did. I didn't sing silly songs either. I just taught him stuff he was gonna need to know in the future.

Leon gazed up at me out of his bouncy seat.

"You're a good listener, bro," I said. "Wanna learn how to skype?"

When Nate appeared on the screen, Leon squealed, and I asked, "How did you do on the admissions test?"

"Terrible," he answered. "I passed."

"What did you do that for?" I said.

"I couldn't help it," said Nate miserably. "I knew all the answers."

It didn't really surprise me. Nate is smarter than the average Dude. And he never met a test he didn't like.

"Don't worry," I told him. "There's one thing that Einstein Academy doesn't have: the Dudes! We'll find some way to convince your mom what a good influence we are."

Then *my* Mom came in with dragon fire in her eyes, and I closed the laptop quick.

Apparently she'd called Mrs. Gutierrez to see if maybe her brother the contractor (remember Uncle Miguelangel who built Teresa's treehouse?)—would put up the swinging bridge for free if the PTA could raise the $2000 for the bridge itself.

"$2000 for a playground bridge?" I asked.

But Mom didn't answer that. Instead, she told me Mrs. Gutierrez had said that Teresa had said that it was Ryan Maguire's idea to break the bridge.

"That's not fair!" I jumped in to defend Ryan. "The whole fourth grade was on that bridge."

When I explained Operation Wall of Flesh Mom's nostrils flared.

"Tyler Hamilton Reynolds, are you telling me you boys were *trying* to see how many students it would take to break the bridge?" she demanded.

"Well, when you put it like that…"

"You'd better go to your room while I try to get over being mortified at what you and your friends have done," Mom said, dragging Leon out of his bouncy seat and away from my destructive influence.

I looked up "mortified" online and discovered that it means, basically, being so embarrassed you wish you were dead, which, I guess, was an overstatement.

I *didn't* have to guess who Mom meant by "your friends"—but I did have to warn them.

I used my computer to send a quick text to Deven's phone:

//Dragon breathing fire. Do not approach the dojo.//

Then, because I didn't want Mom to overhear us, I switched from skype to email with Nate.

T—*Does your mom know what my mom knows?*

N—*The bumble bee got dragon's smoke signals.*

That was a yes. (Like everything else, Nate had taken the code thing pretty seriously.)

T—*Is it bad?*

N—*She buzzed: "This would never happen at Einstein Academy."*

Whoa. Was she calling Sherwood kids dumb or saying the Einstein kids were too snooty to join a decent wall of flesh? Either way, a broken playground made the school look bad. And the fact that the Dudes broke it didn't make *us* look like heroes either. I didn't know what the Dudes could do about it now, though.

Then I got another message from Nate.

N—*"He who wishes to cross the bridge must balance victory with sacrifice."*

Huh?

I was about to write back when I remembered where I'd heard those words before.

It was something Sensei had said in a scene from <u>Ninja Wars</u>, first season. The ninjas had to repair damage from an earthquake they'd caused before they could cross the Bridge of Vision to rescue Jade from the Void. It was a great ep., mainly because of all the cool destruction during the earthquake, but I could see what Nate was getting at. Who says you can't learn anything from screen time?

I wrote back.

T—*Oh wise Owl, we must take responsibility for our screw up. How can we fix the bridge?*

Nate must have been way ahead of me because he responded right away with a picture off the internet of something called a monkey bridge. His message said:

N—*We're going to need some rope.*

11 Dudes At Work

That's where the sacrifice came in. We had to use the three big ropes from the dojo. We took a clothesline from Deven's house too.

"Nani won't be happy," said Deven.

But we were taking responsibility for the consequences of our actions and saving the PTA a load of money in the process. That was bound to make the Dudes look good. I just hoped it would be enough to sway Mrs. Howe's decision about private school.

The trick was to get the bridge built without anybody interfering, and Ryan knew the perfect time—Arts Festival weekend.

The Arts Festival was a city-wide event. There was a kids' art show (which was bound to feature three- or four-hundred paintings by Jayden Reynolds). Judging was in the community center on Saturday morning, so most of the parents, including my mom, would be there.

There were also outdoor exhibits all over town. You could tell they were done by real, professional artists by how weird they were. There was a lady in the park wrapping sweaters around trees and a guy drawing pictures of litter on the sidewalks with chalk. Someone had hung buckets and watermills in the fountain at City Hall to make wet art. Someone else was painting giant plaster pigs—farmyard art, I guess. When one broke, a photographer swooped in to take pictures of the rubble art.

The Sherwood Arts Committee was even giving out these cardboard frames to look through and "make any part of town an art experience." (Deven had been inspired to frame a half-eaten roti and his dad's golf pants.)

Anyway, Ryan figured, with so much to see around town, nobody would be on the school playground during the judging, so we met there on Saturday morning for Operation Monkey Business.

We had all seen the monkey bridge picture, but Nate had drawn detailed sketches to help us build it. We'd also spent yesterday at the dojo, practicing knot-tying under Nate's supervision.

The bridge was essentially one rope to walk on with a rope on either side about waist height to hold onto. We'd use the three big ropes from the dojo for that.

The clothesline was to tie each of the handrail ropes to the walking rope for stability and, hopefully, to keep kindergarteners from falling through.

Each of us had our job:

Nate laid out the big ropes and used anchor knots to tie them to the end posts where the old bridge used to hang. Then he tightened the ropes using several pulleys from his set.

Meanwhile, Connor and I tied the railings to the footrope with pieces of clothesline. Ryan cut those pieces for us with his camping hatchet.

Ryan's dad had sent him that hatchet for a birthday present, and Ryan had been dying to use it. Since they had the same birthday, Connor had gotten a flint-and-steel set at the same time—you know, like you use to strike sparks to make a campfire. Mrs. Maguire thought both presents were dangerous. I don't say she's right, but, maybe it's just as well there was no need for Connor to start any fires on this project.

Anyway, Ryan was cutting the clothesline with a *thunk, thunk, thunk* against one of the posts of the big toy when suddenly, between *thunks*, we heard something we didn't want to hear. It sounded like Deven shouting "TERESA!"

By the way, Deven's job was *lookout*.

"WHAT ARE YOU DOING HERE AT SCHOOL HEADED TOWARD THE PLAYGROUND?" he yelled at the top of his voice.

Don't worry. Ryan had thought of everything.

"Quick!" he whispered. "Begin Operation Seal Screen."

He and Connor grabbed a big blue tarp and threw it over the half-built bridge just as Teresa rode into view on her pink and white bike. Teacup barked and wiggled in a little basket on the front.

"I was just taking Teacup for a ride," Teresa said, as if that was a perfectly normal thing to do.

She looked from Ryan to the tarp and narrowed her eyes.

"What are you up to?" she asked.

The tarp used to cover Ryan and Connor's dad's motorcycle, but I'd borrowed Jayden's paints to paint a seal on it this morning. The seal had long whiskers and a happy smile, and in my opinion it was a pretty good portrait of Sammy the Seal, the mascot of the Sherwood Elementary Seals.

Maybe it was too good because Teresa said, "*This is why you were talking about 'seal harbor' the other day!'*

Ryan didn't let it shake him. He smiled like he wasn't holding a hatchet behind his back and nodded at old Sammy.

"That's right, Teresa," he said. "We're working on a little outdoor art for the Festival."

"It's not finished yet," Nate added, pulling a paintbrush out of his hair and pretending to dab at Sammy's flipper.

Teresa harrumphed.

"You were supposed to register at the Community Center," she said.

With her Uncle Miguelangel on the Arts Committee and her dad's paint store a sponsor of the Arts Festival, I guess Teresa figured she was in charge.

"Gee, we forgot to register," said Ryan.

"Shucks darn!" threw in Connor for good measure.

Teresa shook her head like she didn't know what to do with such forgetful boys. Then she said, "Oh well, I guess I can ride down and do it for you."

"Uh,...thanks?" I said. At least it caused her to leave.

We all breathed a little easier when Teresa was gone. We flipped the tarp back off and finished the monkey bridge in no time. And it didn't even look like monkeys had built it.

I had to admit Nate had the whole thing planned beautifully. We couldn't have done it without him. Of course, if this plan didn't work, we might have to start doing *everything* without him.

We were just about to try out our creation when we heard Deven's voice again.

"HELLO, UH...OFFICIAL PEOPLE!" he hollered.

I reached for the tarp, but Connor and Nate were standing on it. It was too late to hide anything anyway because a whole crowd of people were rounding the corner of the school building.

There were men in suits and women in colorful, scarves and hats. And, with them, was one (well paid) guy in a bird suit: Art the Owl, the mascot of the Arts Festival. They were followed by a photographer and Teresa.

"See!" she said, jabbing her finger at us. "I told you there were kids with an outdoor exhibit."

A portly man stepped forward. He was wearing a ribbon on the lapel of his suit that said "Judge". He looked down at a clipboard he was holding.

"Your registration is incomplete," he said.

He frowned down at the clipboard then looked up at us. "I have no title for your work of ...rope art."

I looked at the monkey bridge. It was a little uneven but looked sturdy. The blue tarp on the ground kind of gave the impression of water underneath with a very happy seal swimming through.

"We call it The Bridge of Vision," I said, giving Nate a high five.

"Excellent," said the judge, scribbling it down on his clipboard.

A woman in a bright red suit and a wide hat stepped forward. I thought she looked kind of familiar.

"This would make a wonderful picture for the Sherwood News," she said.

"Yes, Mayor," said the photographer who lifted his camera.

"Stand on the bridge with me, Art," ordered the mayor. "You too, Carl," she said to the Judge.

Carl didn't look anxious to try the swinging bridge, but the mayor was game, even in her high heels. She tip-toed right out to the center of the rope just fine. Carl joined her on one side, and then Art the Owl struggled on.

The giant bird toes of his costume were getting caught in the clothesline, and we were all laughing—even the grown-ups—when suddenly we heard a loud *CREAK!*

The ropes swayed. I looked at Nate, but he was looking at the posts.

Then I remembered the *thunk, thunk* of Ryan's hatchet into one of those posts.

With another loud *creak* and then a *CRACK!* the bridge sank suddenly and hung swaying about six inches above Sammy the Seal's face.

The mayor grabbed her hat.

Carl screamed.

Art fluttered.

The camera flashed.

And people rushed forward to help evacuate the Bridge of Vision.

"ART COMES IN FOR A LANDING!" read the caption next to a picture that made it look like Art the Owl was trying to fly from danger. Carl and the Mayor didn't look too happy either.

By the time the picture ran on the Sherwood Weekly News online the next day we knew the truth.

11 Dudes At Work

The monkey bridge had held. And it wasn't Ryan's chopping that had caused the collapse either.

It was old age—the playground's not the mayor's. The wood had gotten brittle. The weight of the Mayor and the Arts Festival judge and Art the Owl had caused the posts to pull loose from the bolts that were supposed to hold them to the slide platform. In other words, the climber wasn't safe.

My mom and Mrs. Howe were thrilled to find out the playground was a death trap!

See, they'd been embarrassed when they thought their sons had helped destroy school property. But, if the big toy was too old anyway, we'd actually done the school a valuable service by proving it—and contributed to the arts at the same time.

"The Dudes are very creative," Ryan pointed out, "plus enriching and engaging!"

In fact, I figured the Dudes were looking like the kind of fine, upstanding citizens any mom would want her son to go to school with. We could probably relax for the rest of the summer.

12 The Dudes and the Dads

I was relaxing in the shade, reading, when I heard the sliding door open and footsteps on the deck.

"Come out and see how tall the grass is," I heard Mom say.

Then Dad's voice said, "Wow! I didn't know they'd done all this."

Dad was home from his business trip!

"They've been *doing things* all summer," Mom said darkly, "while you've been at the office or out of town."

"That's good, isn't it?" asked Dad. He didn't sound so sure, though.

"The boys need supervision," Mom said. Her voice sounded a little ragged. "I've been so busy with the baby and now the playground committee that I must be losing my mind. Today I was going to make cookies,

12 The Dudes and the Dads

but I was out of flour. I could have sworn I had a full bag in the pantry, but..."

"Honey, honey," Dad cut in. "Why don't you go in and get some sleep while Leon naps? The boys are fine. Building a treehouse is good, wholesome, outdoor fun, after all."

I heard Mom go inside.

Then Dad called, "Boys?"

I dropped my book and scrambled out of the tent on the highest platform.

"Hi, Dad!" I said.

"Hi, Dad!" echoed Jayden from the middle platform. He was looking out the screened window of another tent. The lower platform had a tent on it too.

Yep. We finally had walls.

After the Bridge of Vision fell, the Dudes had taken our ropes back and rebuilt the dojo. (Though we still owed Deven's grandmother a clothesline.) But, the truth is, it didn't take long to build up our balance, strength and skill. After that we wanted shade and...other things.

"It was a great idea putting these tents in the trees," Dad said.

"We had to," I explained. "After we built the dojo, we were out of wood."

Dad laughed. "That's what I call ingenuity," he said.

"Come up and play!" called Jayden.

"I'd like to, sport. But, right now, I've got to get the grass mowed for your mother," said Dad. "The noise won't bother you boys, will it?

"Not at all, Mr. Reynolds," called Ryan, popping his head out the door of the lowest tent.

"I like noise!" added Deven, from the middle tent.

And Connor yelled, "I'm good!" from the highest tent.

Dad shielded his eyes from the sun. "Are all your friends here?" he asked.

"Sure," I said. "They're always here—except Nate. He has Computer Camp."

"No wonder Meg's so tired," Dad muttered, heading toward the garage.

12 The Dudes and the Dads

The Dudes grinned at each other and went back in the treehouse.

We heard the lawnmower start up, then the distant droning as Dad mowed the front yard.

I was typing a description of the Bridge of Vision into the Chronicle when I heard the lawnmower noise get louder. That meant Dad had passed through the side gate and was starting on the back yard. After that, the noise grew louder and then softer as Dad passed slowly from one end of the yard to the other, cutting his way from the deck to the...

"Whoa! The cord!" I screamed, throwing myself out of the middle tent and nearly falling headfirst before I caught a branch and managed to sling myself out of the tree and across the yard toward the shed.

"Dad! Wait! Stop!" I yelled frantically.

I don't know if he heard me, but I saw his eyes widen as he stared at something over my shoulder.

I turned in time to see Deven zip from the top level and Flying Kick the shed at high speed! We couldn't hear the sound of him slamming into the shed over the growl of the engine, but we saw him release the handle and slide goofily to the ground to lie in the path of the mower.

Dad hit the kill switch. He stared at Deven for a minute without saying anything. Then he turned to me.

"What's all this about, Tyler?" he asked.

"You can't mow any closer to the shed!" I said.

Deven had folded his arms over his chest like a corpse, but he was peeking with one eye.

By now the other dudes were crawling out of the tents.

"Yeah, Mr. Reynolds," said Ryan. "Just hold on and let me move the cord."

Dad looked from me to Ryan. "The cord?" he asked.

"It's right here," said Ryan, lifting an extension cord out of the tall grass by the shed. "I can hold it out of your way while you mow this area," he offered. "I don't want to unplug it because the fridge will stop running."

"Fridge?!" Dad's head jerked in surprise. "What are you talking about? Where do you have a fridge?"

12 The Dudes and the Dads

Dad's gaze followed the cord from where it came out the shed door, along the ground, through Ryan's hand and up the tree trunk like a snake. The cord went in the first tent where we had a power strip and a mini-fridge from Deven's dad's college days. It was stocked with three kinds of soda from Ryan and Connor's house. We also had an old TV from Nate's house and a Game System for playing *Zombie Bash II*.

From there, another cord stretched across the gap to the middle tent. That's where we had our air conditioner. It was really just a pan of water with a fan to blow across the top. Nate had explained how the evaporating water would cool the air, and it worked. The middle tent was a lot cooler than the other two.

Ryan and Connor only had two outdoor cords, so the top tent was pretty low-tech for now. I had brought out a stack of books and comics. And I could type or listen to music on battery power. When we got another cord, we were going to put in a charging station and speakers and maybe a microwave for popcorn.

When we were done showing Dad all the stuff, he wiped his forehead with his wrist and said, "Maybe things *have* changed since my day."

Then he unplugged the extension cord and finished mowing the lawn.

That night at dinner, Dad said, "I had a little time to think this afternoon."

I guess he thinks while he mows.

"I've been thinking you're right, Meg," he said. "The boys need some good old-fashioned outdoor fun."

Mom looked up from her plate. "I don't remember saying that," she said.

Dad raised his hands and nodded as if he was agreeing with her. "I've been so tied up with work, I haven't spent enough time with Tyler and Jayden this summer," he said.

"What are we gonna do, Dad?" I asked, getting to the point.

"I thought we could go backpacking," he answered, winking at Mom like it was her idea. "Do you think we

12 The Dudes and the Dads

could get those tents down out of the trees for a guys' weekend?"

"Oh, boy! Sure!" I said. I was about to say something about the tents when Jayden interrupted.

"What about Leon?" Jayden pointed out. "He's a guy."

"Yes, he is," said Mom, smiling over his head at Dad. "But he's too little for big boy camping. He'll have to stay home with me," she said.

Actually, she looked pretty excited, considering she wasn't going anywhere.

"Sure you'll be all right on your own?" Dad teased her.

"You sure you'll be all right on your own with Tyler and Jayden?" Mom countered.

Dad laughed like that was a joke.

"We'll invite Nate and his Dad along and make a real adventure of it," he said. "It may be our last chance now they're thinking of moving."

I stopped breathing.

"What do you mean, moving?" I gasped.

Dad looked uncomfortable. "Well, Henry let slip they're looking at apartments in the city—to be nearer Nate's school."

"Oh, did Nate get an acceptance letter?" asked Mom.

I felt sick. This couldn't be happening.

"He got high marks on the entrance exam," Dad told her. "All that's left is the interview."

Then Dad turned to me.

"What do you say, Tyler. Are you up for a camping weekend with Nate?"

Before I could answer, Jayden jumped in.

"I want to bring a friend too!" he said. "I want to bring Jello."

"You don't have a friend named Jello," I said harshly.

"Yes I do, and he wants to come."

"I'm sure it will be fine for Jello to come too," said Mom hastily, before a fight could start. She winked to let me know she knew it was an imaginary friend.

12 The Dudes and the Dads

I decided to play along so we could finish dinner. I had some calls to make. Emergency—all Dudes on deck!

On Saturday morning, Dad and I were still trying to roll up the tents and stuff them in their bags when Nate and his dad drove up in Mr. Howe's compact electric car—the one he and Dad carpool to work in when Dad's in town.

Nate got out wearing a long-sleeved safari suit and a hat with mosquito netting draped from the brim all the way around his head.

"Mom says bug repellent has endocrine disruptors," Nate explained.

Nate's dad had ergonomically designed backpacks in the trunk and Deven in the back seat.

"Deven has never been camping," Nate explained giving me the high sign.

Deven nodded. "My dad calls everything outside the golf course 'the rough'," he said.

My dad shrugged. Then he and Mr. Howe both started shoving at the tents.

Meanwhile, Deven showed us his imitation of what we were going to look like carrying the backpacks up a mountain. (It involved a lot of panting for water and wrestling with Bigfoot.)

While Dad and Mr. Howe loaded the packs and tents into the trunk of our sedan. Nate and Deven and I loaded the most important supplies—the snacks for the drive.

"My grandmother made me bring a sack of potatoes," said Deven.

I hefted the sack and groaned.

"They're heavy because they are full of water," Nate explained. "If we roast them in the fire, the steam inside could expand suddenly, causing them to explode."

"Nani packed grenades?" said Deven. "Cool!"

Dad walked up and cast an eye over our array of chips and doodles.

"That looks like a lot for four kids," he said, just as Mrs. Maguire drove up in her minivan.

12 The Dudes and the Dads

"Oh, you'll never get there in that," she insisted, tossing Dad the keys. "Take mine. It's the least I can do to thank you for getting my boys out of the house this weekend."

"Tha...that's okay," said Dad faintly.

While Mrs. Maguire was chasing down her sons for their goodbye kisses, Dad turned to me.

"Did I mention that the tents belong to Ryan and Connor?" I said.

It was all part of our secret plan, of course. We'd already shown Mrs. Howe a thing or two, but Mr. Howe hadn't yet experienced how awesome the Dudes are.

"What better way to recruit him to our side," Ryan had said, "than by getting him alone in the woods and surrounding him with Dude-ness?"

As we piled into the minivan with the two dads, I figured it couldn't miss. Look out, Nature, here come the Dudes!

13 Dudes in the Woods

My dad wasn't kidding about "old-fashioned" fun. The dads didn't let us bring any games or phones or entertainment of any kind. Clearly, in the old days, fun was all about being bored.

"No more music!" Mr. Howe said with a shudder as he locked our gadgets in the van. After a four-hour drive, I guess he'd had all he could take of Deven's "Digital Dudes Party Mix."

So we were living the life of the pioneers. I'm serious. The first thing we had to do was use an outhouse. That's all they had at the trailhead.

The rest of us just held our noses, but Ryan shook his head and staggered back from the door. "I'm not going in there."

"A composting toilet works just as well as the one in your house," Nate's dad explained.

13 Dudes in the Woods

"The one in my house doesn't have *spiders*," said Ryan, shaking his head. "I'm not getting trapped in there with them."

In the meantime, Jayden had realized that Jello wasn't with us and started wailing.

Turns out, Jello is *not* an imaginary friend.

"We'll do something with Jello next weekend, Jayden. I promise," said Dad desperately. Then he broke out the marshmallows and Jayden got one before we even got on the trail.

After that, it was like something out of an explorer's journal. The trail was long and rocky. The packs were heavy, and our feet were sore. Somebody was always dying of thirst or starving to death—Connor, mostly. (And, if you think Connor's scary when he eats, you should hear his stomach growling like a cougar when he doesn't.)

There were other dangers too. Ryan went off the trail to answer nature's call and got stung on the leg by a swarm of killer bees (that Nate said was actually a plant called nettles).

On a rest break, Connor found a snake that had the dads pretty worked up until it turned out to be rubber. (Yeah. Deven is the kind of guy who brings his own snakes on a camping trip.)

The worst was when Jayden found a shiny "rock" that turned out to be a fat slug. Without modern-day conveniences like baby wipes he had to live with slug slime on his fingers—which meant that we all had to live with him complaining about the slime on his fingers and trying to wipe it off on us.

It was late afternoon when we finally got to the campsite. It was primitive camping, which means no outhouse. (Which was just fine with Ryan, of course.)

First, we set up the tents. There were three tents and two dads. Nobody wanted to sleep with the dads, so all the Dudes piled into one tent to see if we could fit.

We couldn't. Okay, so maybe we were taking the togetherness thing too far. But it was important to show Nate's dad what good friends we were.

While we were putting the tent back up, Nate pointed out that the *dads* could share a tent. Then we boys could divide up between the other two and stay with our own kind.

For some reason, the dads laughed at this brilliant reasoning. At least they were in a good mood. Anyway, I ended up sharing a tent with Ryan and Nate. Connor, Deven and Jayden shared the other tent. That way no brothers had to be together either.

"Man, it's hot," Connor complained, crawling out of the tent. "I wish we had our air conditioner."

Then Dad told Mr. Howe about Nate's air conditioner for the tree house.

"That's an innovative idea," said Mr. Howe to Nate.

The Dudes grinned at each other.

"On the same principle, it should be cooler by the lake," Nate pointed out.

"Whatever you say, Nate," said Ryan. "Let's go."

He turned to Dad. "Jayden can come too, Mr. Reynolds," he offered. "We'll save him from drowning."

For some reason, Dad didn't want to take him up on that—which was really too bad because saving a little kid from drowning sure would have made the Dudes look good.

"Jayden can stay here with Henry and me," said Dad. "We're going to get set up to make dinner."

The other guys galloped down the hill to the lake, but I hung back.

This was part of the plan. While the Possum (Dad's code name) and the Gecko talked, I would do some ninja spying to find out what Mr. Howe was thinking. Then the Dudes could counteract it...somehow.

I just needed an excuse to hang around...

"Hey Jayden," I said. "Show me your rock collection."

Jayden agreed and started digging in his pockets.

I sat down on a log a little way from the campsite so I could see and hear everything, It's been my experience that grown-ups forget you exist pretty quickly if you don't keep interrupting them. This time, I would turn that to my advantage.

I had to keep an eye on the lake too. If the Dudes did something terrific I wanted to point it out so Mr.

13 Dudes in the Woods

Howe wouldn't miss being impressed. At the moment, though, I tuned in on what the dads were saying:

"How's the house-hunting going?" Dad asked.

"We've looked at a couple of apartments," Mr. Howe answered.

Uh-oh. This was serious. On *Househunters*, people only look at three places before they choose one and move in!

"Will you feel safe in the city?" Dad asked.

"The suburbs aren't that safe anymore either," said Mr. Howe. "Remember those prowlers that struck on Memorial Day?"

Drat! Foiled by our own ninja stealth! I turned away and caught a glimpse of the guys down at the lake.

Ryan, Connor, and Deven were throwing rocks in the water. Nate seemed to be measuring footprints. I wondered if the Dudes could catch Bigfoot and whether that would impress or repulse Mr. Howe.

Say something, Dad! I thought. *Tell your friend not to go. Make your own destiny.*

"We'll miss you," Dad said. "Meg and Trudy have been working on this playground thing together. And who will I carpool with?"

Carpool? Come on. Why can't grown-ups express themselves like kids do?

I glanced down at the lake shore to see Ryan and Connor had dropped their rocks and begun pounding on each other. See? That's expression!

Jayden showed me two gray pebbles, a stick, and a bottle cap from his first pocket. I admired each item while the dads rummaged in the backpacks. Then Dad started telling Mr. Howe about the dojo, which was good, because I figured that was one of the Dudes' most awesome achievements.

"And they had everything plugged into the shed," Dad was saying. "I didn't even know it had electrical outlets."

Mr. Howe tossed Dad a box of matches. "Sounds like it would make a nice home office," he said.

Dad laughed. "That's not what I thought when I nearly mowed over the cord!"

13 Dudes in the Woods

Great. Dad *had* to bring up the possibility of electrocution.

Meanwhile, Jayden pulled out an acorn, a piece of bark, and a bedraggled beetle who took the opportunity to make a break for it. Some rock collection.

The dads began walking around the campsite, collecting sticks and dry leaves for kindling. I figured they probably could have gotten plenty from Jayden's pockets, but I didn't want to say anything and remind them I was there—especially after they started talking about the night of the fireworks.

"Can you believe they were running naked in the sprinklers?" Mr. Howe asked. "I never would have done something like that as a boy."

Then Dad said, "It was probably Ryan's idea. He's a natural leader,...unfortunately."

"I do wonder whether these 'Dudes' are a good influence," said Nate's dad, adding, "I don't mean Tyler, of course."

Dad frowned, but it was hard to tell whether he was frowning because I *was* a bad influence or because he didn't know how to start a fire. He started building a tiny teepee out of twigs.

"Nate has so much potential," Mr. Howe was saying. "Trudy and I have tried to enrich his free time, but we can't seem to find projects that engage him."

There's that word again. What does 'engage' even mean? I wondered.

"Did you know, he's started losing games in Chess Club?" Mr. Howe went on. "And he won't practice his recital piece on his oboe. Instead he plays tunes from some video game. I don't even know where he got the sheet music for 'Zombie Bash'."

It was *Zombie Bash II: After Party*, which has a much better soundtrack than the original. But I didn't correct him because of how I was undercover.

Besides, I was surprised to hear Nate was screwing up his activities. Maybe something really *was* wrong. Come to think of it, he'd screwed up failing the admissions test too. Was it possible Nate secretly *wanted* to go to Einstein Academy?

14 Dudes Slam Dunk

I tuned out the Dads and started listening to the voice inside my head. I realized I'd never asked Nate if he wanted to stay. Maybe the Dudes were un-enriching him. Maybe getting engaged to Einstein was what he *wanted*.

Nate's dad was squinting at the instructions on a pack of freeze-dried spaghetti. "I didn't bring enough camping food for this crew," he said. "Luckily, Deven's grandmother gave me a sack of potatoes to roast."

Dad was still kneeling over the fire he wasn't making.

"Meg made me bring a jumbo pack of hot dogs too," he admitted.

Mr. Howe chuckled. "Seems like they knew something we didn't," he said.

"That wouldn't be a surprise," said Dad. "All these business trips have kept me out of the loop."

He leaned in like he was gonna tell a secret. "A few weeks ago, all of my black socks went missing," he revealed.

"Really?" said Mr. Howe. His gecko neck stretched forward with interest.

I gulped and looked at Jayden in case he was about to announce how I'd 'helped' with the laundry on Memorial Day. But he was holding something under my nose.

As my eyes tried to focus on it, I hoped it wasn't a turd. It turned out to be a chunk of moss.

"It's soft!" said Jayden, stroking it like a bunny.

I nodded and patted his pet moss while I listened to Dad's sock story.

"I didn't dare tell Meg," Dad was saying. "She's got enough to worry about already. I had to buy socks while I was in Cleveland and slip them into my drawer when I got home."

I was surprised and a little impressed that Dad would do something so sneaky.

Then his teepee collapsed, and he sighed. "Of course, this sort of thing never used to happen before the Dudes," he said. "But I guess you can't pick your kid's friends."

"But you can choose his environment," Mr. Howe argued. "I'm hoping that, at Einstein Academy, Nate will find kids who are like him."

I looked down the hill to where the guys were clowning around—all except Nate, who had found something dead on the shore and was using two sticks to dissect it. I had to admit Nate *was* kinda different. I couldn't imagine the Dudes without him. But, for the first time, I wondered: Was *he* happy with *us*?

Down at the lake shore, Deven was grabbing at his legs, pretending to be stuck in the mud. In a minute he was no longer pretending and had walked right out of one of his shoes which had been swallowed completely by the thick ooze.

What was Nate thinking as he watched Deven hop around on one foot. Did he wish he had smarter friends? Would he 'engage' with those enriched kids at Einstein Academy?

Dad was now shredding the trail map to use as a fire starter. I hoped we wouldn't need it to get home.

"You know, Henry," he said, "friendships are very important at their age."

"You're right," said Mr. Howe, measuring bottled water into a pot. "I got that pulley set for Nathan last year, but he didn't take it out of the box until his friends wanted to make a dojo." Mr. Howe sighed. "I want Nate to live up to his full potential, but I also want him to be happy."

I realized that's what I wanted too. The question was: what did Nate want?

About that time, Deven leaned over to take off his other shoe and tottered into the lake with his clothes on. Connor and Ryan kicked off their own shoes and followed suit, laughing and splashing each other.

My hopes fell when I saw that Nate had turned his back on the Dudes and was hiking back up the hill.

"What's going on, Nate?" asked his dad. "Did you get tired of playing with the other boys?"

Nate took off his safari hat to reveal a sweaty, smiling face.

"Nope," Nate explained. "I just wanted to leave my watch in the tent to keep it safe from raking broadsides."

Mr. Howe's eyes got as big as, well, as a gecko's, and he asked, "You found someone to play Trafalgar with you?"

"Of course," said Nate, pulling his swim goggles out of his backpack. "Come on, Tyler. The Dudes are waiting."

Trafalgar was a splash-battle game that Nate invented, and raking broadsides were one of the strategic maneuvers. The game was based on the real battle of the British Royal Navy against the French and Spanish fleets in 1805. He learned about it in his independent study on the Napoleonic Wars. (I have to give Mrs. Howe credit here for forcing Nate—and, thus, the Dudes—to learn such useful stuff.)

The Dudes had played Trafalgar in the community pool a few times, but this would be our first time in open water. And I didn't want to miss it!

"Come on, Jay!" I shouted, jumping up. "Wanna learn how to be a cannonball?"

Then I pelted down the hill after Nate with my little brother following.

Behind me, I heard Mr. Howe say, "*Be* a cannonball?" before he and Dad came running after us.

Well, Dad finally got the fire started. It was a good thing, too.

Since he'd told us to pack only essentials none of us had brought a change of clothes. So the Dudes and Jayden sat around the fire in our underwear, waiting for our clothes to dry and our potatoes to explode (which they didn't because Nate's dad had poked them like you're supposed to).

Deven used the flashlight to re-enact the water fight with shadow puppets, and Nate laughed so hard he fell off the rock he was sitting on.

Then Dad passed out the marshmallows and we crawled in our sleeping bags.

The next morning, Nate made Deven a shoe out of tree bark. Then we all tramped back to the car, damp and mosquito bitten. It was just about the best weekend of our lives!

I guess Mr. Howe thought so too. On the drive home, he told my dad that, if it were up to him, he'd let *Nate* decide where to go to school.

Nate and I grinned at each other. I knew what he would choose.

Then Mr. Howe went and ruined it by saying, "Of course, Trudy's the one who'll make the final decision."

Nate and I groaned. Changing the world, one parent at a time, was slow going.

15 Dudes At Play

True to his word, Dad invited Jayden's friend, Jello, over for a playdate the next weekend.

It turns out "Jello" is really Cello—short for Marcello. So, chalk it up to a preschool misunderstanding.

When Cello got to our house, it was like having another Jayden running around, same height, same clothes, same mania for justice.

They spent like an hour deciding what their "super names" were going to be. (They settled on Super Red and Super Blue—creative, huh?)

Then they hung jackets on their heads by the hoods and ran around the yard so their "capes" would fly out behind.

Dad was in charge because Mom had an emergency meeting of the playground committee.

15 Dudes At Play

"Go ahead, honey," Dad had said when Mom left. "I haven't spent all day with the baby in quite a while." He jiggled Leon in that way he has that makes Leon squeal and Mom frown, but she went out the door anyway.

I found it interesting to note the differences between Mom and Dad's parenting styles. For one thing, Dad doesn't worry so much about screen time. So I was using my computer to work on the Chronicles. It had been a busy summer for the Dudes, and, with only a couple weeks left, I wanted to get all the tales typed in before school started. I discovered it's not that easy to describe the dojo in words. And forget about Deven's chicken dance! (You'll just have to use your imagination.)

When I left my room to get some lunch, I discovered that the living room had been transformed. The cushions had been pulled from the couch and propped up around the dining room table. Sticking out on one side was a pop-up Thomas the Tank Engine play tent. A climb-through tube led to a second "room" composed of several old sheets stretched between the mini-basketball hoop and Mom's exercise bike.

As I came nearer, dart guns thrust suddenly out of the cracks between the cushions. From inside the tent a voice thundered, "Intruder alert!" Then there were some tremors in the tube, and my little brother's head popped out from under the sheets.

"Hi Tyler!" said Jayden. Then his face got all serious. "Stay away from the Supercave," he warned me.

I stared at him. "The what?" I asked.

Jayden crawled out and stood up. Behind me, a sofa cushion flopped down like a drawbridge and Jello—I mean Cello—emerged.

"This is the Supercave," said Cello seriously, standing beside Jayden.

"You mean, like the Batcave?" I asked.

"A Batcave is for Batman," Jayden explained patiently.

Cello rolled his eyes. "We're supers, not bats," he said.

15 Dudes At Play

I tried not to laugh. Dad had told me to make Cello feel welcome "like *my* friends always were."

"The Supercave has our supercomputer and all our sensors and weapons and a-rangs," Jay told me.

That last one took me a minute. (If you take "bat" away from bat-a-rang...)

"Right," I said, playing along. "Well, uh, good job there, supers."

"Come on, Super Red," said Cello, crawling back under the protection of the super sheets.

"We gotta go wait for the Super Signal," Jayden explained. "There may be trouble in the city." Then he disappeared into the Supercave.

I shrugged and moved on.

In the kitchen, Dad had Leon in one hand and a bottle in the other. Leon's face was dripping, and Dad's shirt was wet.

"I guess he's not used to being fed by me," said Dad, switching off the kitchen TV, which had been on the all-news channel. I had noticed that, for Dad, news didn't seem to count as screen time. Neither did Mariners games.

I also noticed he didn't automatically wipe the remote like Mom does, though there appeared to be some kind of goo on some of the buttons as well as on his coffee mug and his watch.

I made a sandwich and wolfed it down. Leon watched me while deftly avoiding Dad's comical attempts to sneak the bottle into his mouth. Maybe the little guy wanted a sandwich.

About that time, there was a knock. I heard the pounding of super feet and flapping of super capes in the hall. Then: "Bad guys beware!"

Yep. Ryan, Connor, and Deven had arrived. Unfortunately, Nate was with his parents on the way to Einstein Academy for his admittance interview.

After the camping trip, Mr. Howe was ready to forget private school. But, according to Nate, Mrs. Howe had argued they "shouldn't close the door on an opportunity." She was even missing the Playground Committee meeting in order to drive over with Nate and his dad for the interview. I guess proving the playground was decrepit hadn't exactly convinced her that Sherwood School was better than Einstein Academy.

So Nate was spending Saturday dressed up with the rockets combed out of his hair in order to impress the Academy's headmaster. I had a bad feeling that this interview was going to seal the deal, one way or another. And the Dudes were helpless to do anything about it.

My thoughts were interrupted by Leon's squeal of delight when Ryan, Connor, and Deven invaded the kitchen.

"Here's another super-dude!" said Ryan, holding out his hands to the baby. "Let me teach him to fly, Mr. Reynolds."

"Uh, no thanks, Ryan," said Dad, holding Leon tightly. "I was just going to try to put him down for a nap."

He turned before leaving to say, "Jay and Cello, your super lunch is on the table."

The Dudes crowded around, eyeing the little kids' sandwiches.

Jayden and Cello didn't bother to sit down at the table. Cello opened the bread and ate the smoked turkey lunchmeat first. Jayden did the same thing. Then they each stuffed their dry bread in their mouths.

"Interesting technique," said Connor.

"Want me to teach *you* how to fly?" asked Ryan, eyeing the Flying Kick out the window.

But Cello responded quickly, "You're not a superhero. *We're* superheroes."

"Maybe I'm a super-*villain*," said Ryan. (I have to admit his evil grin was pretty convincing.) "I have superpowers, you know," Ryan added.

"You do?" said Jayden and Cello together.

"Sure," said Ryan. He looked around the room. "I can run so fast that I can get that apple off your plate without you even seeing me move from here," he said. He gave a wink to Connor, who was standing behind Jayden near the table.

"No you can't!" said Cello. He and Jayden both stared hard at Ryan.

"I just did," said Ryan with a showman's smile.

The little boys turned around to find the plate empty.

"Wow!" they said together.

Then Connor bit into the apple with a loud *crunch*! Ryan slapped his forehead.

But Jayden whirled on Connor. "How did *you* get the apple?" he demanded.

"Um...Ryan ran over and handed it to him, of course," I explained hastily. "I guess you didn't see it because you don't have super-fast vision like I do."

"Wow!" the four-year-olds said again, impressed with both Ryan *and* me.

About that time, Dad passed through the kitchen, wiping his brow.

"I got him down!" he said, pumping his fist in triumph. (I never saw Mom do *that* at naptime.)

I noticed Dad was carrying his laptop along with the baby monitor, and I wondered if maybe he was gonna play video games in the dojo. But, through the kitchen window, I saw him go out the side door, and across the yard toward the shed.

Then I was distracted by Connor doing his imitation of Mrs. Fenski from third grade, who was almost the same thing as a mad scientist.

"Mwah-ha-ha! I have altered this device to control the minds of men," Connor said, holding up the TV remote.

He pointed it at me and commanded, "Pat your stomach and rub your head."

I let my eyes go blank and did what he said.

Then he pointed it at Deven and said, "Dance like a chicken."

Deven was happy to oblige.

Then he pointed it at Ryan and said, "Act like a robot."

I thought maybe Ryan wouldn't obey his twin brother, but he did. He acted like a robot that was crossing the room to attack Connor.

Connor quickly pushed the "off" button and set the remote down on the table.

Of course, Deven didn't want to be left out.

"Hey! I've got a superpower too," he said, and the little kids turned to him. "I can make this noise that will break your eardrums if you hear it!"

Uh-oh.

Of course, Jayden just had to ask: "What does it sound like?"

Before I could stop him, Deven let loose with a horrible piercing yodel that shook the glass in the kitchen windows!

16 Dudes S-O-S

Jayden and Cello stampeded outside...passing Dad on his way in, his face dark.

"You boys need to play *outside* now," Dad growled as he rushed past us toward the nursery. (*Now* he sounded like mom.)

As we spilled outside, we could hear Leon, still squalling, over the monitor that Dad must have left in the shed. At least *Deven* had stopped wailing. Jayden and Cello stood in the yard facing us.

"They're real super-villains," said Cello.

"Yeah," said Jayden.

"We're the Legion of Dudes!" said Deven. "No—the Dudes of Doom!"

But Cello wasn't laughing. "We have to fight them!" he said. I saw a gleam in his eye.

"They're onto us!" I yelled. "Run!"

16 Dudes S-O-S

The Dudes scattered all over the yard. Jayden and Cello ran around, swirling their capes.

"Good can always defeat evil!" shouted Jayden.

"You'll never defeat me!" said Ryan, leaping out from behind the hydrangea bush.

Jayden swung a punch that missed him by a mile, but Ryan threw himself to the ground like he'd been walloped. Jayden stopped, his eyes widening.

"You must have superpower punches!" groaned Ryan, scrambling away like he was scared.

As Cello swung his cape Connor grabbed the Cursed Enemy and swung himself backward.

"Whoa! They *are* powerful!" Connor called, clinging to the flour sack.

"Don't worry," I said, "I'll roast them with my invisible fireball." I cradled empty air in the shape of a ball between my hands. Before I could throw, the four-year-olds screamed.

"To the Supercave!" Jayden yelled, and they stomped up the deck stairs and disappeared inside.

When Jayden and Cello were gone, the Dudes cracked up. It was just too easy.

In no time, the half-size heroes came back for more. Only this time I noticed something sticking out of the top of Jayden's waistband, dragging down on his shorts as he walked. It was the remote control from the kitchen. He whipped it out like a ray-gun and pointed it at us.

"Now you will do as I command!" he said.

I looked at Ryan, who winked. "Curses!" he said. "Who let the do-gooders get hold of our most powerful weapon?"

"Close your mouth, villain!" said Jayden, pushing a button.

Ryan shut up.

"Put up your hands," said Cello.

We all put up our hands.

"Now walk!"

Ryan and Connor and Devin and I marched obediently down the yard until they told us to stop.

"We're putting you in jail," said Cello.

Ryan cackled. "We'll be back!" he promised. "You know we villains always escape."

"That's why we're putting you in Forever Jail," said Jayden.

I had to admit they had thought this through.

"Now, go inside," said Cello, motioning toward the shed.

Playing along, we all trooped into the shed, which was mostly empty now that we'd used all the wood. I could see Dad's laptop and a tape measure he must have left on the floor. Over the baby monitor, we could hear him singing a lullaby to Leon.

Then the door shut behind us.

"Seal the door," said Cello's voice.

"Yeah," Jayden answered. There was an ominous click. Then nothing.

"Did they leave?" asked Deven.

"Boost me up!" said Connor. He climbed on Deven's back to see out the high window over the door. "They're going inside!" he reported before he fell off.

"Hey!" said Ryan, trying the door. "It won't open!"

"They must have locked it somehow," I said, trying to remember how the door looked on the outside. "And there's no handle in here."

"Stand back," ordered Connor. He ran to the back of the shed. Then he ran forward and kicked the door—just like the police do on TV.

It didn't budge.

Then Connor threw his shoulder at the solid wood.

"Ow!" he howled.

"Stop that before you break yourself," Ryan ordered.

"We're trapped!" said Deven, coughing and squeezing his neck like he was suffocating.

"Relax. We're not in a submarine," I pointed out. "There's plenty of air coming in the cracks."

"But we've gotta find a way out," said Connor.

We all naturally looked to Ryan for a plan.

He thought for a sec then said, "Well, it's a prison escape, so...we dig a tunnel!"

We were pretty excited about that idea until we realized we'd left most of the tools in the treehouse. All we had were a couple of rusty screwdrivers, and the tape measure. Also, the floor was cement.

16 Dudes S-O-S

Deven freaked out and grabbed up the baby monitor. "Mr. Reynolds, can you hear us?" he called. "We're in the Forever Jail!"

"Dude," I said, "that's *still* not a walkie-talkie."

Over the monitor, we could hear Leon making fussy squeals that didn't sound at all sleepy.

I warned the guys, "It might be a long time before Dad comes back out here."

There was no sign of Jayden and Cello either. They were probably back at the supercave polishing a-rangs. I sat down on the floor. The windows were too small to escape through, but they were big enough to let in the sun, and it was getting hot.

"I wonder what Dad was doing in here," I said, tapping idly at the computer.

Ryan looked at me with a gleam in his eye.

"Ninjas," he said, "we're trapped and there's no way out. But one of our number is on the outside. It's time for Operation S-O-S."

Meanwhile, this is what was happening at Einstein Academy. (Nate told me all about it later, so already you know we didn't die in the shed):

Nate and his parents were sitting on a bench outside the headmaster's office, waiting for their appointment.

"The important thing is to show how much you care about this interview... and Einstein Academy... and your future!" Mrs. Howe reminded Nate as she straightened his collar for like the gazillionth time.

Mr. Howe felt a buzz and pulled his phone out of his pocket.

Mrs. Howe frowned at him for getting a text at this most important moment in his son's life.

But Mr. Howe didn't notice because he was frowning at the screen.

"*Hawk, Tiger, Monkey, and Chicken imprisoned in Temple,*" he read aloud. "*Cricket holds the Key?*"

Mr. and Mrs. Howe looked at each other in confusion. But Nate was thinking fast—well, really at his regular rate, which is plenty speedy.

16 Dudes S-O-S

Just then, a stuffy lady came out of the office and told them that the headmaster was ready for "Nathaniel", and his parents should wait here.

Nate stood up and followed her into the headmaster's office. Then he strode right up to the desk and spoke urgently to the stuffy man sitting there.

"I need to use your phone, sir," he said. "There's an emergency at my dojo."

It was a lucky thing Dad had Mr. Howe's number listed in the contacts on his computer—or maybe it was destiny. Either way, it wasn't too long after we sent the text that Dad showed up to open the door. He was still jiggling Leon.

"There's a call for you from Nate," he said, handing me the phone. It had goo on it.

And that's how the Owl saved the Dudes from the Forever Jail and how the Dudes saved the Owl from Einstein Academy at the same time.

17 Dudes Dough Op

I know what you're thinking. Nate was home-free, so why continue the story?

I sure wasn't worried that night at dinner when Mom told us all about the playground committee's idea for a walk-a-thon to raise money.

"We got local businesses to sponsor us for each pupil-lap," she said.

"What's a poop-a-lap?" Jayden asked.

It's handy to have a little brother to ask the stupid questions so you don't have to.

Mom explained that the money would be earned for each *lap* around the playground that was walked by a *pupil*.

"I told Trudy that you and your friends would be glad to help out," said Mom, by which I knew that she hadn't forgotten her mortification.

17 Dudes Dough Op

"No problem," I agreed. I was in a good mood now that Nate was in no danger of getting into Einstein Academy. (That headmaster got pretty huffy about letting Nate use his phone for emergency dojo business. Or maybe it was the way Nate rushed out afterward, forgetting his interview entirely.)

Leon made a few happy gurgly noises as he looked at Mom and chugged his bottle.

Mom smiled down at him as she asked, "How did the playdate go?"

"I think Jello—I mean Cello—had a good time," Dad answered heartily.

"We put the bad guys in jail," Jayden piped up.

Mom nodded absently.

I expected Dad to tell her how the shed was a dangerous trap that should be torn down, but he seemed to have learned entirely the wrong lesson from the day's adventure.

"I've decided I want to spend more time with the kids," Dad announced. He leaned forward with this crazed—I mean excited—look in his eyes. "I want to be my own boss and work at home—you know, make my own destiny!" he said.

He looked around at Jayden and Leon and me. "It would mean less money," Dad warned. "But we'd save some on daycare when Mom goes back to work."

Mom frowned as she lifted Leon to her shoulder. "Where would you work?" she asked. "I suppose the boys could share a room..."

Before anyone could scream, Dad interrupted her.

"Actually, I'm going to turn the *shed* into my office!" he announced, with the same grin I'd swear I've seen on Ryan's face sometimes. "It has electricity and good light," Dad told her. "In fact, it wouldn't really need much work except to put real knobs on the door," he added, with a glance at Jay.

"I measured it today," Dad explained. "And the kids even tested the wifi."

This time he glanced at me.

Then he looked anxiously at Mom. "Well, what do you think?"

Just as she opened her mouth Leon burped.

17 Dudes Dough Op

Mom laughed. "Well, *I* think it's a wonderful idea too!" she said.

Then we all laughed at the same time, like a sitcom family.

Dad told Mom, "It was really Henry Howe who first realized the shed could be an office."

"You should thank him," she said.

"Yeah," said Dad, catching my eye. "I think I owe him one."

On Sunday afternoon, the Dudes were hanging out on Ryan and Connor's back patio. It was Mrs. Maguire's day off, so we were making use of the jumbo bag of generic cereal she had bought on her weekly run to the Warehouse Store.

Nate and I were sitting on the picnic table watching Connor toss Choco Puffies at Deven's open mouth. (Nate had calculated that Dev was catching about 40 percent, but Choco Puffies cost eighty percent less than the name brand cereal, so we were actually saving money.)

Meanwhile, Ryan was staring at the Big Toy on the other side of the chain link fence.

When they'd first moved in, Mrs. Maguire had liked the way she could keep an eye on her boys when they were on the playground. When she'd seen what kind of crazy stunts Connor liked to do she had changed her mind about wanting to watch, but it was still convenient for Ryan and Connor.

"They're tearing it down in a week," said Ryan.

The Big Toy had been around since before the Dudes were in kindergarten. I was going to miss it.

"It's apocalyptic," said Nate, echoing my thoughts.

Deven gave him a cross-eyed look. "What's acoptalixic?" he asked as cereal bounced off his face.

"Apocalyptic means the destruction of everything," Nate explained.

"Like in *Zombie Bash II*," Ryan added.

"Oh, right," said Deven.

Nate said, "The PTA has chosen new playground equipment, but it's expensive. My mom says the walk-a-thon may be only the first of several fundraisers. It might be months before we have enough money. And we won't be able to use the playground at all until the new equipment is installed."

We all knew what that meant: playing Duck, Duck, Goose in the lunchroom every day. The Dudes fell silent, contemplating a world with no recess.

Then Ryan said, "We'll just have to raise *all* the money at the walk-a-thon!"

Nate did the math. "Taking into account the total pledges, I calculate that we would need to complete 3500 pupil-laps," he said.

Deven sniggered and repeated "Poop-a-laps" a few times. But the rest of us were stunned.

"That's like...700 laps a piece," Connor figured. "It'll take us days."

"Actually, it would take the five of us close to thirty hours," Nate corrected.

"Well, we don't have to do it all by ourselves," Ryan reminded us. "We've just got to get a lot of kids to show up."

He began to pace, crunching cereal balls with every step.

SAVE THE DUDES

"The PTA is putting up posters," Nate explained, "but it's one of the last weekends of the summer, and a lot of people are on vacation."

"Or have *fun* stuff to do," I put in.

"We'll be walking all night," groaned Connor, collapsing in a lounge chair.

"Not if we make kids *want* to come," said Ryan.

"Right," said Connor. "Step right up for your chance to waste a Saturday walking around and around the soccer field," he announced. "Kids will be dying to help us."

"Grown-ups waste Saturdays all the time," Nate pointed out, "doing chores, exercising, shopping. What motivates them?"

"Coupons?" Connor said.

"Peer pressure?" I guessed.

"Cameras!" said Deven. "Mom says, whenever there's an important trial at the courthouse, flocks of people show up for the chance to be on TV, even if they have to watch the trial."

"Then we'll make a movie!" said Ryan. "Like the one Nate made about his Lego battleship."

"It was actually a destroyer," Nate corrected. "But I still have the video software, and I could borrow my dad's camera again."

"I don't know," said Connor. "A walk-a-thon video is kind of lame."

Ryan elbowed his twin in the ribs. "We're not gonna film the walk-a-thon," he told us. "The walk-a-thon will be the *audition*."

Then he rubbed his hand through Connor's hair in that way Connor hates.

"You were right after all, little brother," he said. "Kids will be *dying* to help us. Because we're gonna make a zombie video!"

This announcement was followed by a chorus of cheers and hoots from the Dudes. Connor even did a back-flip.

"Such a topic should appeal to a wide range of students," Nate predicted. "And it has the added advantage of using a large number of actors."

"He's right," I realized. *Zombie Bash III: Disco of Doom* has hundreds of zombies in the first level alone.

There's even a level with a stadium full of the undead. This raised a question.

"Um, you're not thinking of filming it at my house, are you?"

I breathed easier when Ryan said, "Your house isn't scary enough." Then he gestured over the fence. "We'll film it at the doomed playground."

He quick laid out a plan: "Nate will be the cameraman, of course," he said. "Tyler and I will be the zombie hunters. And we'll need as many zombies as we can get."

Connor immediately began throttling Ryan, which wasn't unusual. But the wheezing and limping were new. He leaned in to take a chomp out of living flesh.

Ryan blocked his bite then swung an invisible machete to decapitate his brother.

Meanwhile, Deven dropped to the ground and started dragging himself along like his legs had rotted off.

Right about that time I noticed that Ryan and Connor's mom was staring at us out of the laundry room window.

"Oh hi, Mrs. Maguire!" I called, giving her a cheerful wave.

She shrugged and went back to her laundry like she hadn't seen a thing.

Finally, Ryan got Connor in a headlock. "Of course, we need to get the word out fast to as many kids as possible," he said.

"We could tell the guys at Ninja Camp," suggested Connor from under Ryan's arm.

"And there is Chess Camp and Junior Orchestra and Rocket Workshop…" Nate mused. For once I was glad his parents had him in so many activities.

"I see guys in golf and tennis at the Club," put in Deven.

"What about girls?" said Ryan.

We all looked at him. Connor slid out of his brother's grasp and tripped over a potted geranium.

"What *about* girls?" he asked.

"We can't let *boys* do all the work," Ryan explained. "Now how can we get the word out to a bunch of girls?"

But there was really no question.

"Tell Teresa!" we said in unison.

Then we got to work planning the whole thing.

The next time Mrs. Maguire passed by a window, assuming that she dared to look, she would have seen something scarier than any of Connor's stunts: the birth of Operation Undead.

18 Dudes-A-Thon

As far as the walk-a-thon went, Operation Undead was a huge success.

Mrs. Howe put up flyers at the Community Center and sent out emails offering free popsicles.

The Dudes spread the word more discretely. After all, we didn't want a lot of little kids finding out and wanting to be in the movie. Undead kindergarteners might be scary, but we all agreed they couldn't pull it off as actors.

On the Saturday of the walk-a-thon, the Dudes showed up early to help organize.

"We're happy to do our part for the school, Mrs. Howe," said Ryan. "You know, Sherwood's students are 'Destined for Greatness'," he added, quoting the banner she had made and which was taped to the school gate.

"Of course," agreed Mrs. Howe. Then she turned away, dabbing at her eyes like maybe the dust from the soccer field had got in them.

Deven was working the sign-in table with his dad, mostly because none of the other Dudes wanted to work under Mr. Singh's stern gaze. It seemed to make Deven a little nervous too. Of course, if a little kid signed up, he was just supposed to remind them to count laps. But Deven's *secret* mission was to give the high sign to the big kids who were in on the movie thing. Nate had suggested he come up with a subtle code phrase that would sound normal to the adult volunteers but would remind a kid of exploding zombie brains.

When Kent Meadows stepped up to print his name, Deven said, "If you do 25 laps, it will blow your mind!" Then he made an explosion sound for good measure.

Mr. Singh shook his head at his son's silliness.

"You'll get a free popsicle," he informed Kent seriously.

"What about the..." Kent started to ask, but Deven jumped out of his seat, knocking his chair over in the process.

"Walk! Don't talk, man!" Deven urged him, nearly shoving Kent away from the sign-in table. "Time's a wasting!"

Mr. Singh stared at his son.

"We've got a lot of people in line here, Dad," said Deven innocently. "I'm just trying to keep things moving."

His father nodded and waved over the next pupil.

"Am I in the right place?" asked a fourth grade girl.

Deven lowered his voice. "Are you here for the invasion?" he asked.

"Invasion?" asked Mr. Singh, overhearing.

"Woodworm, Dad," Deven answered. "That's why the playground is *rotting* and its *guts are falling out!*" He yelled the last part with an exaggerated nod so the other kids would get the message.

"You have to walk 'til you're *dead on your feet!*" he announced. Then he turned back to the girl. "I'm sure walking 25 laps will make you a *real star*," he said, wiggling his eyebrows.

When she left, Deven sighed and started to sit down in his chair. Of course, he had forgotten he'd turned it over and ended up dumping himself on the ground.

Mr. Singh watched his son scramble out of the dirt. "I believe your grandmother may be right that you are eating too much sugar," was all he said.

It had been Ryan's idea to require a kid to do 25 laps to be in the movie. Nate had calculated a fifth grader could walk that in a little over an hour. If enough older kids showed up, we'd have the money in no time.

The walking course encompassed the playground and the soccer field combined. PTA volunteers stood around the edges, cheering on the kids as they plodded by. I couldn't help noticing the jolly smiles of parents, who chatted and drank coffee from paper cups. I guess they figured they had tricked their kids into exercising. I would have been outraged if we didn't have our own sneaky scheme going on.

18 Dudes-A-Thon

Over by the climber, Nate was counting laps and logging them down next to each kid's name.

Ryan gave each of the little kids a high five and sent them over for a popsicle. Big kids got a handshake. If they'd done twenty-five laps, Ryan would slip them a secret note in the process—real smooth. The notes had the date, time, and instructions for the zombie filming.

Connor and I were the last stop, passing popsicles from Mrs. Maguire's big cooler to kids who were on their way out the gate. I was also keeping an eye on the Playground Committee. We didn't need them overhearing conversations about decapitation or decaying flesh. If kids were talking about the movie, I was ready to get something in their mouths, quick.

The moms were standing behind Connor and me, so I couldn't help hearing what they were saying.

"There's certainly been a good turnout," I heard Nate's mom say.

"The free popsicles were a great idea, Trudy," my mom replied happily. I knew she was glad the Howes were staying so Mrs. Howe could keep doing all the work of the Sherwood PTA.

SAVE THE DUDES

I was feeling pretty good too. For every kid that finished his laps, there were two more coming in. My fingers were even getting frozen from handing out so many popsicles, and Dad had already run to the store twice for more.

I peeked behind me. Leon was napping in his stroller. Jayden was running around punching invisible enemies. Dad was looking at his phone, but he had his arm around Mom like he was proud of her. Mom was smiling—in relief, probably, that her work with the Playground Committee was almost over.

I expected Nate's mom to look pleased too, but something was wrong. Her ruby red lips were all pinched together and her eyes were darting around the playground, more like a suspicious fox than a busy bee.

"I wonder if we have a problem with youth sports in this community," said Mrs. Howe, with a frown. "I've never seen so many children limping."

Alarmed, I turned back to scan the field. Kids weren't *talking* about zombies. They were getting into their roles too early! Some were limping or lurching. A few were holding their arms out in front of them.

"They're just dedicated," I said hastily as a guy passed me with a glazed expression and a trail of drool hanging from his mouth. "This school means a lot to us kids," I added.

"They'll walk 'til they drop!" said Connor, putting a popsicle in the guy's limp hand.

Then Mom had the solution. "I bet they're getting hungry," she said. "It's almost lunchtime."

Mrs. Howe turned to mom, just missing the sight of Joey Ortiz pretending to suck the brains out of Xander Flint. (Not much of a meal, if you know Xander.)

"Maybe we should have provided sandwiches," Mrs. Howe worried.

Dad sighed. I guess he figured he'd have to go back to the store.

Anyway, in about six hours we had earned all the money we needed for the new playground. I could tell Nate's mom thought her posters had done the trick.

She gathered all the adults so she could make a little speech.

"This is the most successful fundraiser we've ever had!" she declared. "Thank you to the PTA for providing popsicles and sandwiches and to Tyler, Ryan, Connor, Deven, and Nate for their diligent efforts. (We were so diligent, none of the Dudes had walked a single pupil-lap! Besides that, Ryan had handed out 137 secret notes. So Operation Undead was a go.)

Mrs. Howe fluttered her hand in front of her face as if to dry the tears on her mascara.

"It's so meaningful to me," she said, "that my last project as PTA President has ended so successfully."

Uh-oh.

"What does she mean by 'last project'?" Connor asked.

I felt a cold weight like a popsicle in my belly as Mrs. Howe answered that question.

"I'll miss you all next year," she said, "when I'm homeschooling my son Nate."

19 Dudes Apocalypse

"Homeschool? No way!" I said. It was the next morning already, but I still couldn't believe Nate's fate was sealed—that the Dudes' work to make our own destiny had failed.

"How could she do that?" Ryan asked. "Your mom's not a teacher."

"You don't have to be," Nate explained. "There are all sorts of lesson plans online. Mom's already looked into it."

We were sitting around the Maguires' picnic table loading darts.

"But your mom loves Sherwood School," Connor protested.

"Yeah, it's the Dudes she hates," put in Deven, sliding a clip into place.

"It's not that," said Nate. "She says she wants to 'provide unique learning opportunities' to 'stimulate my creativity' with 'engaging projects'. I guess she thinks I'll have more time for that stuff if I'm not wasting so much of the day at school."

"...and with the Dudes," I added.

"The problem is we don't have time to do anything about it," said Ryan, snapping the laser sight on his rifle.

"Yeah, school starts in less than two weeks," I moaned.

"You guys might as well start doing things without me," said Nate. "Maybe I should go home."

"No way," said Ryan, handing Nate his safety goggles. "You'll take part in the apocalypse if it's the last fun you ever have!"

The Dudes stood up and grabbed our gear.

"Besides, we need a cameraman," said Deven practically.

"I wonder what the *new* playground will look like," said Connor.

19 Dudes Apocalypse

He was carrying a bag of licorice in the crook of his elbow and a small, round watermelon under his arm. Still, he managed to climb over the chain-link fence one-handed.

Deven followed Connor into the schoolyard, and I passed him the rifles.

We could have gone around through the school's front gate, but we had to stop by the Maguires' anyway to get the watermelon, so climbing over the fence was a shortcut.

"The fort on the Big Toy was the first roof I ever fell off!" said Connor, adding nostalgically: "I got six stitches." Then he pointed to his chin. "And I got this scar running up the slide."

"Yeah," said Ryan. "Mom says they're tearing it down because it finally got dangerous for everybody else." He slung himself over the fence wearing a crossbow and a backpack full of extra darts. His hatchet hung from a belt loop.

"They're tearing this playground down on Monday," I said. "So it's a good thing we're filming today."

Nate nodded. "I agree. It's possible our film could have historical significance," he said, hefting a bucket of blood.

It was early on a Sunday. Mrs. Maguire would sleep late, we hoped. But, just in case, Ryan had shut all the blinds on the back side of the house.

By the time we had our gear in place, kids were already straggling through the gate wearing old clothes and practicing their growls.

Luckily, the Dudes had planned ahead and were totally organized.

It was my job to inspect the costumes. I had brought a bunch of Dad's old work shirts for kids that looked too good. But my policy was that you could wear anything, as long as it looked like you'd crawled out of the grave in it.

Therefore, I didn't question why Kent Meadows had been buried in an "I'm With Stupid" t-shirt. And I certainly didn't ask Teresa why she'd apparently been buried with Teacup who was wearing a doggie suit and tie.

When the costumes were approved, I made everybody roll around where the grass was worn away on the soccer field so they could acquire a layer of "graveyard" dirt.

Some of the kids had brought Halloween masks and fake scars. That was helpful.

Connor passed out black licorice to make people's teeth look gross too.

Then Deven squirted everyone with blood—a task, you can imagine, that he enjoyed.

It turns out fake blood is pretty expensive and comes in these tiny tubes at the costume shop. So the dudes had all brought red stuff from our cabinets: ketchup, raspberry syrup, fruit punch. Nate had mixed it up together that morning. It looked gruesome, but it smelled nice as Deven squeezed it out of the plastic ketchup bottles onto our zombie hoard.

When we were ready, Ryan shushed everybody, and Nate started filming a shot of the closed school and the empty playground draped in caution tape. The day was kinda overcast, which was creepy. And the Big Toy, with its weathered wood and tilting bridge posts gave the impression there was nobody left alive to repair it.

Next the two heroes strode onto the scene—that was me and Ryan, wearing camo t-shirts and carrying dart guns. Mine was the Defiance Mega Combat with the sniper barrel. Ryan's was the Omega Point-Position Power Blaster with double action.

Ryan was even wearing his signature cowboy hat. He had a steely-eyed look, like he was expecting trouble. When the first zombie shuffled into sight, we were ready for him.

Now, the thing with video games is how at first you start off nice and slow, blowing the heads off one or two undead at a time. But, by the time you get to the mall, the zombies are coming out of the woodwork—and the GAP and the food court...you get the idea.

Of course, those are virtual zombies. Let me tell you: real ones are a lot harder to control! First off, our zombies were a chatty bunch. Nate tried telling them that the speech centers of their brains were supposed to be destroyed by the virus that had made them undead, but it didn't help. When they weren't talking to each other, they were calling "Flesh! I need flesh!" or "I'm coming to get you!" instead of moaning and hissing like they were supposed to.

Deven even started saying, "I vant to bite your neck!" until Nate reminded him that was for vampires.

And then, in the heat of an attack, when Ryan popped him right in the forehead, there was always some guy who couldn't resist saying, "Great shot!" before he fell down. (Okay, sometimes that was Deven too.)

Unfortunately, the zombie virus seemed to affect kids' brains in other ways. Nate would say, "Spread out," and, instead, they would clump together until you couldn't distinguish one putrefying body part from another. Or he would say "Form a circle," and the kids would just mill around the field like...well, like zombies.

There were gigglers, too. A whole pack of girl zombies couldn't understand that they were supposed to be emotionless. The slightest thing would set them off, and then they'd be staggering around, holding their bellies like their intestines might fall out...

Actually, that might work for the video after all.

Nate filmed everything, just in case. "This kind of movie involves very different challenges than the one displaying my Lego destroyer," he said, watching bullets fly on his camera's little screen.

He was right about the challenges. There were zombies who wouldn't fall down when the darts hit them but kept coming after me and Ryan, or who died but got up and moved so they could die next to their friend.

There were zombies who got hungry and started squirting the blood into their mouths. Well, that was mostly Connor, but it was still annoying. And then there was the fact that the dead zombies (I mean those that had been killed *again* since becoming un-dead in the first place) didn't like to stay on the ground too long because the fake blood was attracting ants.

On top of all that, Ryan and I only had five ammo clips each plus what was in our guns—that's about a hundred and fifty darts total. So we could only keep the action going for two or three minutes before all the zombies had to stop attacking and help pick up darts so we could go again.

On top of the regular action, we had several feature scenes to film—things like Deven taking a crossbow bolt to the chest and sliding backward down the slide or Connor falling off the tunnel tube...and the balance beam...and the cargo net (Dressed up as different zombies each time, of course. We were making a quality picture here.)

Nate did some special camera work too that involved the watermelon and Ryan's hatchet.

The most dramatic, in my opinion, was the scene where Ryan and I stood back to back, spraying out our last darts as the hoard advanced. Nate filmed it from the top of the climber with Deven holding his shirt to keep him from falling.

As the zombies closed in around us, I thought about desperate things like running out of ammo and Nate being homeschooled and cafeteria meatloaf, and I shouted out my frustration

with a battle-cry and a burst of fire before switching to my back-up gun—the Dominator with tactical light—and blasting the last of the undead into oblivion. Now that's acting!

Finally, we filmed the last scene—a slow pan of the entire playground practically draped with bodies and Ryan and me walking away with guns over our shoulders, whistling.

As soon as Nate yelled "cut!' all the zombies jumped up and started wiggling and patting themselves down in case they had ants in the pants. Some bees had gotten interested too by this time, so we didn't have to tell our actors to go home and clean up. Besides, it was Sunday, and some of the undead were late for church.

20 Dudes Deliver

The Dudes met up again on Monday morning in Ryan and Connor's back yard. Uncle Miguelangel's construction workers had just a week to clear the old junk off the school playground and get the new equipment installed before the first recess.

In honor of the occasion (and her day off), Mrs. Maguire had cooked a deluxe breakfast of Toaster Pockets and Choco Moo, and we had our lawn chairs all set up to watch the Big Toy get demolished.

"Where's Nate?" asked Connor, tilting his chair back on two legs.

Deven tossed him a football. As he caught it, Connor tipped over backward into the grass and rolled head over heels out of the chair. It looked almost accidental.

"Nate emailed that he's still working on the movie," I told them.

Ryan nodded. We all knew Nate wouldn't show us until it was perfect. That was just part of the deal with Nate.

"Too bad he's missing the destruction," said Ryan pointing to the bulldozer and dump truck that were parked next to the playground. Several burly guys in hard hats were standing around.

"Why don't they get started?" I asked.

That's when we saw the flashing lights. A police car was driving right up onto the soccer field!

We scrambled over the fence in time to see a couple of familiar cops get out of the car.

"Dude! Those are the cops who chased us!" said Deven.

Ryan grabbed him before he could draw attention by running away. "*They* don't know that," Ryan said, logically. "We were wearing masks, remember?"

"Oh yeah! Ninja-style," said Deven, rolling his shoulders in an overly casual way as we approached the playground. "The Chicken dances, but the Pandas are blind," he said, switching to code.

The older cop was talking to the construction workers while the younger one walked carefully around the Big Toy.

"Better stay back, kids," warned the older cop, whose nametag said Officer Morgan. "This is a crime scene."

"Cool!" said Ryan.

Instead of crunching the climber, the construction crew was huddled around, whispering and looking spooked. The idea that something bad had happened here made me nervous too.

"By the scuff marks, it looks like some kind of fight," said the young cop. "And I found this."

He held up my dad's torn shirt that one of the zombies had worn.

My face turned as green as the drips of paint down the front from when Dad painted our front door. That was evidence, wasn't it? And it would lead straight to my house.

"What's that stain, Racarro?" asked the older cop, pointing to the collar.

"It looks like blood."

"Better see if it matches what the construction workers found," Morgan said grimly.

Ryan looked at me and grinned. "That looks more like ketchup to me, officer," he said helpfully.

"Yeah," I said, relief in my voice, "I'm surprised the ants didn't eat it all by now."

Racarro scowled at us.

But the older policeman narrowed his eyes. "I don't know what you're talking about, son," he said grimly. "But I know dried blood when I see it."

The younger policeman pointed to a trail of dark reddish drips that led up the slide, through the tunnel, and onto its roof. Even I could see that wasn't ketchup.

Officer Morgan laid a hand on my shoulder. "Now, if you boys know something about what happened here, you'd better spill it."

We all stared at the blood.

"Dudes!" shrieked Deven. "One of those zombies was real!"

"It must have gotten up and walked off after we killed it," said Connor.

"They all did that," scoffed Ryan.

But I remembered something else that happened during the filming.

I looked at the baffled police. "I think I can explain," I said.

"I certainly hope so," said Officer Morgan.

For once, an adult wanted to hear the whole story. But, I realized, a picture was worth a thousand words, and a video was even better.

"I can show you digital proof," I said. "But we'll have to go to a friend's house."

Morgan nodded to Racarro, who was writing everything down in a notebook.

"Was this friend involved in the incident?" asked the young cop, his pencil poised over the paper.

I hesitated. Nate's parents hadn't liked the Country Club security guards. What would they say when the Dudes brought the police to their door? Nate was already being homeschooled. Would Mrs. Howe make us stop being friends? Would she decide to move after all?

"Yes, sir," I said, reluctantly. "His name is Nathan Howe."

Making a movie is more than just filming scenes, of course. Nate had put the video on his computer. Then he'd rearranged all the good scenes and cut out the bad ones. For instance, he'd erased the part where Teresa's little dog had put the bite on Ryan, (probably giving him the canine zombie virus in the process). And he'd cut about forty scenes where it was really obvious that the zombie who had just gotten his brains blown out was either laughing or angrily protesting that the dart had missed. Most importantly, Nate had cut out the scene where Connor got a nosebleed and a zombie stopped rampaging in order to offer him a tissue. That's what they call editing.

Nate had worked on the video most of the night, and he had just saved the finished movie when his dad answered the door and found four Dudes and two policemen on his front step.

The police insisted on watching the whole movie as well as the outtakes. That took about thirteen minutes. Yep. If you ever want to know how long it takes two dudes to kill a hundred thirty-seven zombies—some of them more than once—now you know.

And by the way...it was awesome! Nate had converted it to black and white—which made the gore and purple guns look more realistic. And he had added his own eerie oboe music to match the mood of each scene.

There were special effects too. At one point, the Connor-zombie fell down with his head behind the tunnel tube. Nate cut to a scene of Ryan raising his hatchet. Then something rolled fast off the end of the climber and smashed on the ground.

"Eww!" screamed Officer Racarro.

Morgan frowned at his partner, but I noticed him tugging uncomfortably on his collar during the girl-zombie scenes. When Nate went in for a close-up on all those painted nails and wild eyes…Trust me, you don't want to meet Teresa dead!

When the movie was over and the police had left, Ryan threw an arm around Nate.

"Dudes," he said. "this is gonna make us famous!"

I was just glad it didn't put us in jail. But Nate's parents had a few questions.

"Where did you learn these film techniques, Nathan?" Mrs. Howe asked. "And who taught you how to do the special effects?"

"You never had a film production class," put in his Dad. "Did you?"

Nate's eyes bugged and his breath got fast, which, if you don't know him, gives the impression that he has some kind of disease. But the Dudes and I recognized the signs that Nate was juiced about making videos.

"I didn't know any of that stuff before I started," Nate told his parents. "But, the more I worked on it, the more ideas I had. And then everything just fell into place."

Mr. and Mrs. Howe looked at each other and smiled. "It sounds like you were truly *engaged* in this project," said Mrs. Howe. (Huh. So *that's* what that means.)

"I could never have done it on my own," said Nate truthfully.

"The Dudes were happy to help, Mrs. Howe," Ryan explained. "We've got connections." (By which he meant we knew a lot of zombies.)

"Yes, of course," said Mrs. Howe thoughtfully. "I hadn't considered what creative stimulation your peers had to offer." Then she smiled at us for probably the first time ever.

I kinda think that was the moment Mr. and Mrs. Howe gave up on the idea of homeschooling Nate. Apparently, the Dudes were enough enrichment for anybody.

By the time we got back to Ryan and Connor's house, the construction crew had already torn down the Big Toy—fake blood and all. With summer over and school starting next week, it felt like the end of an era.

Basking in the success of Operation Destiny, the five of us headed back to the dojo to relax and plan for the future. For one thing, I'd better learn how to type faster. As long as the Dudes are together, the Chronicles are bound to get longer.

THE END

Thanks for reading! If you enjoyed this book, please send the Dudes some love with a review.

Get Book Two of The Dudes Adventure Chronicles FREE!

It's 5th Grade, and the Dudes are ready to rule the school.

The mission:
- **Inflate the class economy,**
- **Rock down the walls,**
- **Race to the state capitol, and**
- **Take over the governor's office.**

The Goal:
To take possession of the most powerful dart gun ever invented!

You won't want to miss Deven's hilarious election speech, Jayden's Dude-themed birthday bash, or the battle with baby-stealing bandits!

Guard your garden gnome because Dudes are taking over!

Get a free download of <u>The Dudes Take Over</u> here: https://epicspielpress.emilykayjohnson.com/get-book-two-of-the-dudes-adventure-chronicles-free-2/

Or find the paperback and audiobook at your favorite retailer.

Tyler Reynolds has been entrusted with the awesome duty of preserving the legend of the Dudes' epic adventures for all time. He lives with his mom and dad, two brothers, and a dog. He spends his non-screen-time with his four best friends.

Check out his website at **thedudeschronicles.com**

Visit his author page on Amazon.com

Emily Kay Johnson occasionally comes out of hiding to collaborate with Tyler on the dubious project of sharing the exploits of the Dudes with the world. She lives with her husband, sons, and cats in the Pacific Northwest.

You can reach her at **EmilyKayJohnson.com**

Visit her author page on Amazon.com

Please leave a review at your favorite retailer.

Made in United States
Orlando, FL
12 December 2021